# Fantastic Australians

Stephen Gard lives the marginalised life of an un-empowered Anglo-Saxual houseband and platterfamilias. He is unready to discuss deconstructivism, tantric sex, networking or white-water rafting, has never been in Tuscany, or on the fee side of a Writers' Week micro-phone, and is therefore overqualified to write a book about the language of ordinary Australians. He hopes that, if everyone in the future will be famous for fifteen minutes, it won't be compulsory.

# FANTASTIC OFFSTRALIANS

**Key**

1. Bumbaldry
2. Bumberry
3. Burrumbuttock
4. Boobyalla
5. Numbugga
6. Boggabri
7. Boobara
8. Breeza
9. Burpengary
10. Carapooee
11. Condong
12. Doo Town
13. Dunbogan
14. Dunedoo
15. Peedamulla

16. Fannie Bay
17. Fiddletown
18. Finke
19. Galah
20. Ghooli
21. Innaloo
22. Iron Knob
23. Yorkey's Knob
24. Mount Mee
25. Muckadilla
26. Peebinga
27. Pimpinio
28. Poowong
29. Pularumpi
30. Raminea

31. Ringarooma
32. Rooty Hill
33. Sodwalls
34. The Spit
35. Tootgarook
36. Upper Plenty
37. Weerite
38. Wee Wee Rup
39. Nobles Nob
40. Wongawilli
41. Woohlpooer
42. Leeka
43. Missabotti

# FANTASTIC AUSTRALIANS

Stephen Gard

Kangaroo Press

Thanks to Bonds for permission to use the character
'Chesty Bond' on the front cover.

Cartoons by John Shakespeare

© Stephen Gard 1994

Reprinted 1994

*First published in 1994 by Kangaroo Press Pty Ltd*
*3 Whitehall Road Kenthurst NSW 2156 Australia*
*P.O. Box 6125 Dural Delivery Centre NSW 2158*
*Typeset by G.T. Setters Pty Limited*
*Printed by Australian Print Group, Maryborough, Victoria 3465*

ISBN 0 86417 588 4

# CONTENTS

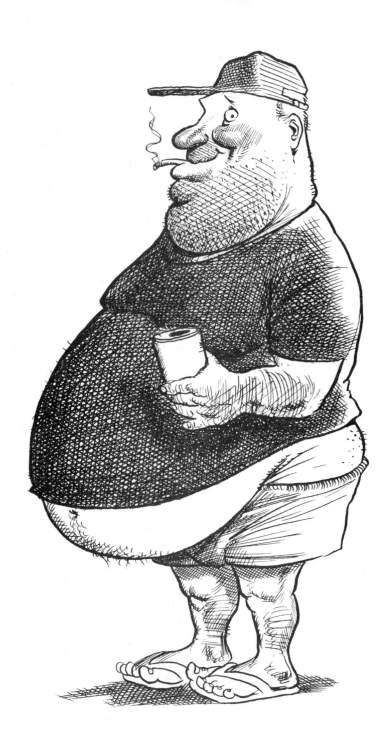

# INTRODUCTION

The one stream of poetry which is continually flowing is slang.
—G.K. Chesterton

In 1770 Lieutenant James Cook took Australia from its original inhabitants by raising a Union Jack over the site of the Kurnell oil refinery.[1] Consequently, Australians are now supposed to speak English. And they do. But the *way* they speak it puzzles the visitor, English-speaking or otherwise. This book was written to catalogue the confusion.

The Australian language is allusive. Its linguistic landscape is crowded with phantoms, pseudonyms, *noms de plume*, fabulous places and personifications. *Hughie, Buckley, Aunty, Bluey, the drover's dog* and *Bandywallop*, not to mention the *Demon Bowler, John Thomas* and *Emma Chissit*, people our speech and confound the foreigner.

Strictly speaking, a *Fantastic Australian* is an imaginary person or place which exists only in our written or spoken language: *Bullamakanka, Cock-Eye Bob, Bunyip.* But others duckshoved their way into this compendium, real things and real people: *bulljoe* and *billycart*, the *bodgie* and the *Balmain Basketweaver.* My original criterion for the inclusion of a word or phrase was that it must live in today's language; yet a number of entries slipped past the wicket-keeper to show that our inventiveness has a

---

1. First Australians present are alleged to have muttered 'Far Kurnell!'

provenance of more than two centuries. There is, for example, an abundance of Fantastic Australians amidst the pages of Sydney J. Baker's *The Australian Language*. A few of them are included here, but many have eternally departed from our lips and eyes.

Within as well, are the elect who have mounted to that summit of mentionedness where their moniker becomes a byword: Australians speak of the *Menzies Era*, but they also refer to the days of *Pig Iron Bob*, or when *Ming* was P.M. Having admitted such candidates to the pantheon—*Kerr's Cur, the Little Digger, the Big Fella*—it seems only fair to include eponyms: *Owen Gun, Hill's Hoist, Victa Mower,* and *parramatta, bowser* and *brumby*. Nor should our solecisms, malapropisms, misnomers and other misbegottens be left out in the cold: *ambleeance, ashfelt, dashhound...* They are surely fantastic. And finally, a place is found for some things which have vanished, yet linger in the language, if only to be summoned amongst the shouts and murmurs of a Trivia Night: *Australia's sons, Dollar Bill* and the *Sanno Man*.

Why is Australian speech so slangy? Why can't we just say what we mean, in clear, dignified English? Perhaps our colonists fended off boredom by making oblique conversation an art-form. Maybe, in a country so drab to its new inhabitants, their speech was the only colourful thing on the horizon and they shaded and stained it accordingly. It might have been an attempt to build a 'nation' of ideas and images, since to build one of either brick or marble seemed such an aching impossibility. The Australian sense of humour is wry, dry and sly. We are amused by the bemusedness of strangers in a strange land. In the spirit of this fretful, clever perversity, some of the definitions in *Fantastic Australians* are circular.

Our colloquial speech has been described as *Slanguage, Strine,* and *The Jack Lang*. It's been analysed and gathered in a number of well-written and thoroughly researched volumes, to which the serious reader is earnestly referred.[2] *Fantastic Australians* is not a work of scholarship. It's more of a rough and ready reckoner, a hip-pocket Who's Who and vulgarian Gazetteer. You're invited to consult it for genuine pleasure and *incentivation*.

---

2. A select bibliography appears at the end of this book.

# A

**Ack-Emma & Ack-Willie** Two wartime lovers, one who liked to rise early, one who often absented himself without leave.

**Adelaide Chinchilla** The pelt of the Brushtail Possum *(Trichosurus vulpecula vulpecula)*, as sold by the hundred thousand to overseas furriers until the endangered animal became a protected species.

**Aerial Ping Pong** The Sydneysiders' contemptuous name for Melbourne's passion, Australian Rules Football, a non-contact code invented by the coach of Australia's first Koori cricket team as a form of exercise. Melburnians refer to Sydney's preferred code of Rugby League as *Mobile Wrestling.*

**Afferbeck Lauder** Author of the instructive *Let Stalk Strine,* that invaluable guide to the correct pronunciation of Australian English. *Nom de plume* of Alistair Morrison.

**Agoniser** Any Australian suburban newspaper is usually referred to as the *Local Rag,* no matter what grandiose title its banner bears. It also often earns a derogatory nickname, usually referring to the tendency of its editor to beat up news where there is none. Thus, any paper calling itself the *Advertiser* will be named the *Agoniser.* Cf. the *Courier Wail,* the *Daily Horror,* the *Terrorgraph* or *Telecrap,* the *Sickly Moaning Herald...*

**Akubra** The characteristic wide-brimmed rural titfer, made of rabbit fur, now universally worn

Akubra

by persons who've never been West of Epping or Bellgrave. (Company brand name.)

**Alf** Archetypal Australian male, i.e. a Philistine, as personified by those self-appointed guardians of the Isaac's Wells of our culture.

**Ambleeance** A *veekle* for rushing *peeble* to *hostible* if they've got *ammonia*, or been *bidden* by a *tryanchula* or *sumpthink*. See also **Fibergayd**.

**Andy** The identity of the Jolly Swagman who invited us to come 'Waltzing Matilda' with him, as revealed by three lines of the song's chorus:
*Andy sang,*
*Andy watched,*
*Andy waited 'til his billy boiled,*
*'Who'll come a-Waltzing Matilda with me?'*

**Ankle Biter** Child, esp. one not yet walking erect. Also: *Rug Rat; Curtain Clinger.*

**Annie's Room** A fob-off; a retort to a foolish or inconveniently-timed question, as in: *'Mum, where's me clean underpants?'* The received response is: *'Up in Annie's room behind the clock!'*

**Anthony Hordern's Tree** Like Myer's, Fossey's, and Buckley & Nunn's, the now-departed department store Anthony Hordern's is an Australian byword. The firm's 'logo' (before such words were in vogue) was a large and spreading tree, and its motto was *While I Live, I'll Grow.* At the summit of the Razorback Range, south of Sydney, grew a grand, look-alike Moreton Bay Fig, which was a landmark for motorists in the days when long, steep climbs were a challenge to the under-engined family sedan. The tree has gone, and folklore insists that it died when the firm went out of business.

**Anzac Button**  A nail in place of a missing button.

**Apostrophe Man**  Hammer of the punctured punctuation of everyday written English; scourge of the ill-planned handwritten sign. The acts of Apostrophe Man are recorded in the *Sydney Morning Herald*'s clearing-house of inconsequentia, *Column 8*. Apostrophe Man fights for truth, justice and the abolition of the redundant apostrophe, which i's wedging it's way into place's where no apostrophe belong's.

**Apples**  The expression *She's apples* means *She's jake*.

**The Apple Isle**  The home of Taswegians.

**The Argonauts**  A unique literary club for children, born 7 January 1941, conducted as a segment within the excellent 'ABC Children's Hour', a lively and intelligent radio program slain by the conquest of the Antipodes by the Cyclops television. Scores of Australia's leading citizens with minds were once Argonauts, and remember their ship and number proudly. (The author was *Palamon 14*, but a slack oarsman.)

**Argus Tuft**  Captain of the legendary football team famous amongst schoolboys, which included the noted Hunt brothers Mike, York and Eric, front-rower P. Ness and fullback R. Sole.

**Arthur**   Obverse of *Martha*; the choices of the confused, beleaguered Australian: *'Garth doesn't know if he's Arthur or Martha.'*

**Arty Farty**   A person or occasion stinking of culture. The antithesis of an **Alf**. Also: *Arts Smarts* and *Smart Arts*.

**Ashfelt**   Black surface of school playgrounds, made of asphalt, where teachers scream at children: *'Stop running on the ashfelt!'* (Lest you fall and injure yourself, and I have to complete an Accident Report.)

**Atlantean Bus**   Double-decker omnibus, which replaced the ageing Leyland Tigers of the Sydney fleet. They've now gone the same route as the **Bondi Tram**.

**Aunty**   The Australian Broadcasting Commission, the government-owned (if not controlled) national broadcaster, personified. Also known as *The ABC* and *The Abe*. Aunty was starchy in her early days, the provider of 'improving' programs which did not pander to the masses. Announcers were reputed to wear dinner suits at the microphone, and spoke Bush House R.P. Aunty's image is more modern today, but she still pawkily defends her autonomy. Announcers now use Balmain R.P.

**Australia Felix**   Once the name of the Colony of Victoria, a happy-go-lucky country.

**Australian Ballot**   A term not used in Australia, to describe the secret ballot.

**Australian Flag**  The tail of a shirt hanging out of the trousers. (Will it be adopted by the republicans, like *Blinky Bill*?)

**Australian Fly Veil**  A hole in the seat of the pants.

**Australian Salute**  A hand waved across the face, to drive away flies.

**Australia's Sons**  The national song, which began:

*Australia's sons, let us rejoice,*
*For we are young and free...*

has been politically corrected to:

*Australians all...*

**Australites**  Mysterious, flying-saucer shaped rocks (tektites), perhaps of extra-terrestrial origin. A.k.a. *Blackfellow's Buttons.*

# B

**Back O'Bourke**  Any remote place; or one more than an hour's travel from the speaker's location.

**Back of a Truck**  Australia's commercial vehicles are neither less robust, nor more badly driven, than those of the rest of the world, but their loads are notoriously insecure:

*Scene:* any pub.
*Macka:* Wanna buy a video?
*Whacka:* I might. Where'd you get it?
*Macka:* Fell off the back of a truck.
*Whacka:* (Furtively) How much?

**Bagman's Gazette**  A mythical publication, avidly read by swagmen and others beyond the pale and quoted as a source of questionable truths and veracious rumours.

**Balmain Basketweaver**  A Balans-chair socialist. A tilt by NSW Labor premier Neville Wran at the chattering but otherwise inactive supporters of his party and its program, who allegedly loll in the trendy harbourside hubburb of Balmain, stringing beads, stitching sandals and munching lotus.

**Balmain Boy**  A dry-eyed, street-wise urchin who has battled his way to the top and can thus face adversity without sobbing on shoulders. A stoic remark by Premier Neville Wran (born and bred in the once working-class suburb of Balmain) whilst subject to investigation by a Royal Commission: 'As you

know, Balmain boys don't cry...' *The Age,*
13 June 1983.

Balmain Boy

**Balmain Bug**  A saltwater crustacean *(Ibacus incisus)*, highly edible, found in Sydney Harbour and its upmarket littoral restaurants.

**Bananabender**  Inhabitant of Queensland. Australian urban folklore insists that bananas grown in this tropical northern state are straight, and that the Queenslander's bent is giving each piece of fruit a quick and wristy two-fisted twist, which gives it the proper shape for selling to the sybaritic citizens of the sinful South.

**Bandywallop**  A non-existent, bushwards hamlet, home of the clodhopping hobbledehoy.

**Bank Johnny**  A passé name for a bank clerk. Most tellers seem to be female these days.

**Barbecue Set**  A coterie of criminals, corrupt authorities, suss celebrities, **colourful racing identifies** and fellow underworld revellers who meet socially.

**Barbie**  Not the doll. A hypocorism (i.e. baby-talk) for 'barbecue'. Used to refer to the social event, as well as the cooking appliance used there.

**Barker's Egg**  Canine faeces, when encountered on the footpath, or more frequently, on the shoe-sole.

**Barney**  Fisticuffs, often merely verbal.

**Barney's Bull**  A bovine with a big bum. To be *all behind, like Barney's bull* can mean that you are either tardy, incompetent, or callipygian.

**Barrenjoey**  A headland at the mouth of

Broken Bay (NSW). A corruption of the Aboriginal word *barrenjui.*

**The Bastard from the Bush**   A countryman who proves himself smarter, profaner and tougher than his city antagonists. From *The Captain of the Push*, attributed to Henry Lawson:

*'Would you care to have a gasper?'*
*said the Captain of the Push.*
*'I'll take the bloody packet,'*
*said the Bastard from the Bush.*

**Beach Inspector**   A municipal officer, employed to safeguard the decency of Sydney bathers when bikinis first became fashionable. He (it was always *He*) was empowered to estimate, and if necessary, measure the coverage of Her (it was always *Her*) body, and could require Her to leave the beach if He considered Her attire inadequate.

**The Bearded Clam**   The female pudendum. The young Australian male boasts of his amorous conquests as *spearing the bearded clam.*

**Beardies**   Glen Innes, NSW, is the *Land of the Beardies*, from two early, barber-starving stockmen. The Beardie Festival is held in November each year.

**Bedroom Mug**   The humble crockery beneath the bed: Also *Thunder Mug.*

**Beggars-in-the-Coals**   Skinny little dampers; flour and water cakes baked amongst the ashes.

Beach Inspector

**Bellbird** The place where Charley Cousens fell off the silo, leaving a forlorn Laurie Chandler. The mythical setting of the ABCTV soap of the same name. Heir of **Blue Hills**; sire of 'A Country Practice'.

**Ben Dover** A mate of **Phillip McCaverty**.

**The Big Australian** Broken Hill, Proprietary. A.k.a. B.H.P., one of Australia's largest companies, a titan in the steel and coal industries.

**The Big Fella** New South Wales Premier Jack Lang (1876–1975), a Labor hero, and a very big man.

**The Big Smoke** Any metropolis.

**Billjim** The poet Henry Lawson's Everyman: Unionist, drinker, swearer, grafter (in its sweat-soaked sense) and salt-of-the-workers'-earth.

**Billycart** Child's go-cart (soap-box racer), made from a fruit box (when such things were wooden), a board and two perambulator bogies, though ball-bearing wheels were prized as well.

**Billy Tea** Tea made in the bush, over an open fire, in a 'billy', a tin pint-pot with a bail and sometimes a lid. The tea is drunk scalding hot, rarely with milk, but often with much sugar. Sacrosanct to its preparation is the whirling of the boiling billy in a vertical circle, at arm's length, supposedly to settle the leaves. Connoisseurs add a handful of gum tips before serving. Today, more folklore than infusion.

**Billywog** Political cartoonist David Low, of **the**

**Bully**, made continual fun of the voluble, diminitive egotist Prime Minister W.M. (Billy, **the Little Digger**) Hughes. Low insisted that the gibes were unmalicious; Hughes called Low a bastard to his face. The Billywog was a supposed children's toy. Low's instructions: *'Blow up with wind until head expands, then release hole in face, whereupon Billy will emit loud noises until he goes flat...'*

**The Bishop**   The *membrum virilus*, from its fancied resemblance to the chess piece of the same name. *'And the same size,'* say some Australian women.

**Bishop Barker**   A tall, narrow glass of beer, named after Bishop Frederick Barker (1845–81), presumably for his lofty stature rather than his liking for lager.

**Bitumen Blonde**   A brunette.

**Bitzer**   Breed of dog, whose pedigree is best described as *bitzer this an' bitzer that.*

**Black Prince**   A variety of colourful cicada *(Cyclochila australasiae)* prized by school-children, who collect 'locusts' during the summer months. Believed by them to be of value to science, and redeemable for hard cash at the chemist's. Other identities: *Green Grocer, Yellow Monday, Floury Baker, Cherry Nose, Double Drummer* and the fabulous *Union Jack.*

**The Black Stump**   A legendary datum, marking the edge of civilisation. Outback Australia begins *past the Black Stump*. There have been many claims about the identity of the original. Also: the State Office Block in Sydney, a veritable Dark Tower.

**Blind Freddie**   Blind Freddie presides over the last court of appeal when the glaringly obvious is in question. *Even Blind Freddie could see that!* is the advocate's usual exasperated scream.

**The Bloke**   The boss; C.J. Dennis' *Sentimental Bloke*; the Deity.

**Blonde-headed, Stompie-Wompie, Real Gone Surfer Boy**   Yeah, yeah, yeah, yeah. A 1963 hit pop-song for 'Little Patty' (Patricia Amphlett), celebrating Surfies, teen love, beaches, bleach and a Neanderthal dance called the 'Stomp'.

**Blood Alley**   Not a place of violence; a much-prized marble, or *taw*.

**The Blowtorch**   Parliamentary weapon for the purpose of payback, e.g. by pitilessly exposing an opponent's rorts, sorts, torts and forgeries, in return for his asking too many astute questions.

**Bluebottle**   A stinging jellyfish (genus *Physalia*) known elsewhere as the *Portugese Man-of-War*. Enemy of Australian surf-bathers, who keep a sharp eye out for its peacock-blue bladder bobbing amidst the waves.

**Blue Heeler**   The Australian cattle dog, a mottled-grey descendent of the Scottish 'blue merle' with a tendency to go for the heels of meter-readers and door-knocking evangelists.

**Blue Hills**   Writer Gwen Meredith created the ABC's long-running radio serial about the outback Lawson Family, set amongst the mythical Blue Hills.

**Blue-Rinse Set**   A coterie of conservative, elderly women, supposedly shockable and censorious, whose badge is their hair, dyed light-blue to disguise its whiteness and thinness.

**Bluey**   A swagman's bundle of personal possessions, i.e. swag, which often had a blue blanket wrapped around its exterior. The expression *humping Bluey* should now become clearer, and less scandalous, to the ears of aliens. Also: a traffic-infringement notice.

**Bob**   Ubiquitous, avuncular Bob appears in the expression *Bob's your uncle*, which means *she's* **Jake**. Also: a shilling, before **dismal guernsey**.

**Bob-a-Job**   Boy Scouts' and Cubs' fund-raising exercise, whereby they went door to door, doing odd jobs for a **bob**. The Guides and Brownies pursued a *Willing Shilling*. The name changed to *Cents For Service* after the arrival of **dismal guernsey**. Nowadays, it's *Job Week*, held during October. Urban folklore says that there was once a householder who commissioned five Cubs to wash, wax and vacuum his car, and afterwards gave them a **bob** to share.

**Bobby**   In **Groperland**, a small beer glass.

**Bobby Dazzler**   An outstanding, pleasing circumstance.

**Bodgie**  A lout; a delinquent youth, adopting a certain style of dress: tight jeans, longish, wavy Brylcreemed hair, leather jacket and pointy-toed shoes. Elvis (pre *Vegas*) Presley in appearance; Marlon (pre *Godfather*) Brando in behaviour. Teenage slang from the late Fifties and early Sixties, the word remains in the language as an adjective for 'doubtful', 'faulty' or 'ill-made'.

**Bogan**  An unsophisticate; a bucolic galoot, visiting town during **bush week**. From the inland NSW river.

**Bogan Flea**  The barbed fruit of *Calotis hispidula*, which cling to wool and cause cursing at shearing time.

**Bogey**  A wash (al fresco); a swim. (Koori)

**Bondi Tram**  An extremely rapid and crowded form of public transport, renowned for leaving intending passengers behind. Hence the expression, *He shot through like a Bondi Tram* i.e. left hastily. The phrase is still in use, though the trams have long terminated.

**Boofhead**  A foolish person. Also: a comic strip character, not noted for his wit, created by R.B. Rudd.

**Boomerang Bender**  A yarn-spinner; a teller of tales which are too true.

**Botany Bay**  The fabled destination of English convicts and other early immigrants, voluntary or otherwise. In fact, there never was a settlement at Botany Bay; the First Fleet chose

Port Jackson, a little further up the coast, for the site of the colony.

**Botany Bay Dozen**   In convict slang, a flogging of twenty-five lashes.

**Bottle-oh**   Primordial recycler who used a direct-selling mode. The bottle-oh drove around in a cart, buying empty bottles from thrifty households. Like the *rabbitoh*, the *milko*, the **garbo** and the **sanno man**, he's vanished from our streets in these do-it-yourself days.

**Bottle-oh's Rouseabout**   A person of no social status.

**Bottom of the Harbour**   A tax-evasion practice of the Seventies. By rapidly selling and reselling, asset-stripping and appointing fantastic directors, a company and its records could effectively disappear—to the 'bottom of the harbour'. Dignified as a 'protest', or 'tax revolt' by **Silvertails** against the government's inequitable tax scales.

**Bourke**   Exclamation of one forced to projectile vomit. See also **Ruth**.

**Bowser**   Petrol reservoir; either a tanker-truck or the pedestal-pump at a service station. From the F.S. Bowser Company of Sydney.

**Bowyang**   The bushman's bicycle clip; pieces of twine tied around the trouser leg to keep the cuffs out of the mud.

**Brass Monkey**   Austral thermometer. Certain days in winter are read off as *cold enough to freeze the balls of a brass monkey*. In polite society: *cold enough to freeze the walls of a bark humpy* or *off a billiard table.*

**Brass Razoo**  Smallest coin in the Austral currency. Value unaffected by decimalisation, stagflation, One Nation or **incentivation**. As in:

*Con:* Can you lend me a few **bob**?
*Ron:* Mate, I haven't got a brass razoo.

**Brewer's Droop**  Impotence arising—so to speak—from the ingestion of alcohol.

**Brian Westlake**  A character invented by lads at Sydney Grammar school, popularised by a graffiti campaign and other sophomoric jackanapery.

**Brick Veneerial Disease**  Architect Robin Boyd's writings about *The Australian Ugliness* brought to everyone's attention the unlovely architectural mish-mash of Australia's cities and suburbs, and made a joke of the Australian Dream, the 'Triple-Fronted Brick-Veneer Home'. In due course, Australians revolted against stodgy conformity and sought to express their taste with more individual designs. See **Federation Home**.

**Bringemebarraback**  Mythical back-blocks burg, burlesquing polysyllabic Aboriginal place-names.

**Brothel Creepers**  Suede boots with thick, corrugated soles.

**Brown Betty**  A pudding of breadcrumbs and fruit pieces.

**Brown Dog**  Anonymous canine exemplar of the extreme. As in the phrases:

*Maurie:* Does he drink?
*Horrie:* Christ, mate, do brown dogs bark?
Or:
*Gaz:* How's the beer at the Withered Arms?
*Baz:* Mate, it'd kill a brown dog and rust its chain.

The brown dog is a red kelpie, a cattle-harrying breed which can allegedly digest almost anything, except a poison bait.

**Brown's Cows**  A legendary herd of ill-disciplined, dawdling bovines, as in: *'Get in line! Youse are wanderin' all over the shop, like Brown's cows.'*

**Bruce**  One of the circle of mates around *'the old Australian stockman, lying, dying. . .'* in Rolf Harris's classic 'Tie Me Kangaroo Down, Sport'. Supporters Jack, Bill, and Fred were asked to return koalas, mind platypuses and tan hides, but Bruce was urged to *'Let me Abos go loose. . . They're of no further use. . .'.* Bruce has joined **Australia's sons** *(. . .let us rejoice, For we are young and politically correct. . .).*

**Brumby**  A wild horse; possibly named after nineteenth century breeder Major James Brumby.

**Bubbly Jock**  And *Bubbly Mary*: The wompoo pigeon *(Ptilinopus magnificus).*

**Buckley**  To *have Buckley's chance* is to have no

chance at all. Perhaps derived from Melbourne retailers Buckley & Nunn.

**B.U.G.A.U.P.** Late in the Seventies, this anonymous organisation, enemy of cigarettes and sexism, devoted itself to the purposeful defacing of advertising hoardings. The original text would be transformed into socially-conscious propaganda. An acronym of *Billboard Utilising Graffiti Against Unhealthy Promotions.*

**Buggery** Not the sexual proclivity; a remote destination. For example: *He lives way to Buggery out past Woop Woop* or: *I wish to God they'd go to Buggery and let me alone.*

**Bullamakanka** Another fabulous hamlet, out beyond **the Black Stump**.

**Bulljoe** A large, belligerent ant, with a taste for toes, and a memorable sting.

**Bull's Wool** Nonsense.

**The Bully** Australian weekly newspaper, the *Bulletin*, founded in 1880 by John Haynes and Jules F. Archibald. Of outstanding historical importance in fostering Australia's growing sense of identity, even making the Brit an object of derision. The *Bulletin* published thousands of 'pars' sent in by contributors around the nation, and thus earned its nickname of 'The Bushman's Bible'. The *Bully* continues today as a somewhat Tory Australian equivalent of *Time.*

**Bundaberg Honey** See **Cocky's Joy**.

**Bundy** An informal unit of measurement, used

outback to estimate the length of a journey by road, assuming that the traveller will drink bottles of Bundaberg Rum as a viaticum. As in:

*Len:* How far is it from Kununurra to Kalgoorlie, mate?
*Ken:* Oh, mate, that's a six Bundy trip.

**Bunyip**  A mythical monster, featuring in many First Australian myths. A dweller in swamps and billabongs.

**Bunyip Aristocracy**  In the 1850s W.C. Wentworth (the First) proposed the institution of an Australian House of Lords, which would require the creation of an Australian Peerage. 'I suppose we are to be favoured with a bunyip aristocracy', sighed Daniel H. Deniehy in the *Sydney Morning Herald*. The phrase has passed into the language to describe **Silvertails**.

**Bush Baptist**  One professing a strong belief, but belonging to no particular religious creed.

**Bushfire Blonde**  A redheaded woman.

**Bush Lawyer**  A strongly-opinionated—and sometimes, well-informed—lay arbiter and loudmouth.

**Bushman's Clock**  The kookaburra.

**Bush Oyster**  A sheep's testicle.

**Bush Telegraph**  A rumour medium. Australia's more popular bushrangers, the 'flash' type, rather than the brutal criminal, obtained news of police movements from admiring small farmers and poorer settlers, and so avoided capture—for a time.

**Bush Week** The annual visit of the hapless hayseed to the **Big Smoke**, usually for the Agricultural Show. During Bush Week, **Bogans** are allegedly sold the deeds to the Harbour Bridge and shares in **Lasseter's Reef**. An Australian who scorns an attempt to gull him may sneer *'What d'you think it is—Bush Week?'* Also: *Wallaby Day*: Saturday, when the bushies come to town to shop.

**Butcher** In the country of the **Croweater**, a small beer glass.

**Butcher's Canary** A blowfly.

**Buttinski** A sticky beak; an unwelcome interrupter. Also: a device used by telephone technicians to tap into a line.

**BYOG** Not a resumé, but a reminder to *Bring Your Own Grog* to a function or hostelry.

# C

**Cactus**   The prickly pear *(Opuntia inermis)* introduced from Mexico (n.b. in S. America) early last century, to the detriment of millions of acres of Oz pasture; controlled finally by the hungry larvum of the *Cactoblastis* moth. Also: the state of being of an unfortunate:

*Shaz:* What'd the boss say about the budget?
*Kaz:* We're cactus.
(From *cacked* = defecated?)

**Callithumpian**   The religious denomination to which most Australians will admit to belonging: a wedding-christening-funeral churchgoer.

**Canning's Little Dog**   A marsupial mouse (Dasycercus cristicauda), mis-named after explorer Alfred Canning (1861–1936).

**Cape Sparrow**   A mosquito.

**Captain Cook**   A look. (Rhyming slang.)

**Captain Cook's Axe**   'It's had nine new heads and six new handles, but it's still Captain Cook's axe.' John Clarke (a.k.a. **Fred Dagg**), *The Sun-Herald*, 2 May 1993.

**Captain Starlight**   Several Australian bushrangers styled themselves 'Captain': Captain Thunderbolt, Captain Melville, Captain Moonlight, for example. Captain Starlight was the invention of author Rolf Boldrewood, and he exists only in the pages of the Australian classic 'Robbery Under Arms'—though there are many opinions about the identity of Starlight's prototype.

**Chaffcutter**  1. Inadequately silenced motor-car. 2. Male who copulates like a decrepit machine. (Sheilaspeak.)

**Chesty Bond**  A jut-jawed he-person, with washboard torso, used to advertise a brand of men's underwear.

**Chinaman**  A ball delivered by a left-handed bowler to a right-handed batsman.

**Chinese Burn**  A playground torture. The victim's forearm is gripped with both hands and the skin twisted in opposite directions.

**The Chips**  A Sydney commuter train, carrying home those who travelled to work on **the Fish**.

**Chloë**  To be *as drunk as Chloë* is to be as drunk as possible. A full-length nude of Daphnis' donah has hung in Young and Jackson's Melbourne pub for decades. Perhaps Chloë is considered to have partaken of every toast proposed on the premises?

**Chocolate Soldier**  A wartime term of contempt for a member of the Militia, an armed force which was not intended to leave Australia, though by 1943 its area of operation extended to the Equator.

**Chuck**  Vomit (verb or noun); perform, or organise: *chuck a mental* (a fit of rage); *chuck a party* (host a celebration).

**Clayton's**  An ironical adjective, e.g. *a Clayton's sickie; a Clayton's sympathy; a Clayton's welcome.*

Clayton's is a non-alcoholic beverage, promoted as a 'sophisticated' soft drink. The highly successful sales slogan was: *Clayton's—the drink you have when you're not having a drink.* The bottle's label confides that Clayton's is made from *a thoughtful and secret recipe known only to key members of the company*, which suggests that, like KFC and Coke, the ingredients include a dash of the old snake oil. . .

**Clean Phil** Sometimes spelt *Fill*. Suburban fugitive. *Clean Fill Wanted* say the hand-painted signs nailed to front fences. This causes a truckload of soil to arrive from a neighbour who is excavating for a swimming pool.

**Cobblers' Tacks** *Bidens pilosa.* A weed with nail-like burrs that stick to the clothing. Also: *Cobblers' Pegs.*

**Cockatoo** A lookout, to give warning of the approach of The Authorities.

**Cockeye Bob** A precipitate, violent storm.

**Cocky Laura** or *Lora*. Playground game similar to *British Bulldogs*.

**Cocky's Joy** Not the bone of a cuttlefish, but a syrup made from cane sugar. Supposedly the staple of the small, impoverished pastoralist. Eaten with **johnny cakes** or damper.

**Colonial Goose** A roasted leg of mutton.

**Colourful Racing Identity** Journalese euphemism for a senior criminal, especially one running a stable of cabinet ministers, police commissioners and journalists.

**Commons**  Ordinary house bricks.

**Connie Agate**  A marble made of marble, much hoarded by schoolboys.

**Cooloola Monster**  *Cooloola propator (Rentz)* is described as 'an aberrant Grasshopper', which neglected getting itself identified by science until 1976. Males reputedly go to pieces during thunderstorms.

**Cornstalk**  An early term for a white born in Australia.

**Country Member**  Objectionable Parliamentary Representative, whether from a rural constituency or otherwheres. As in this parliamentary exchange (in parliamentary language):

*Dick:* Now, I'm a country member...
*Nick:* (Interj.) We remember!

**Cousin Jack**  Cornishman; especially a miner.

**Coward's Castle**  The Houses of Parliament, where one may, from behind the skirts of 'parliamentary privilege', scream the kind of invective which would elsewhere earn one a knuckle sandwich, or a litigious kneecapping.

**Crack Hardy**  To keep up a cheerful appearance in the face of adversity.

**Croweater**  An inhabitant of the state of South Australia, an epithet inspired by the Piping Shrike, proper, on their escutcheon. Also possibly arising from the bleakness of the South Australian interior, wherein are located a large portion of the Nullarbor Plain (tree-less),

Sturt's Gibber Desert (soil-less) and the enormous Lake Eyre (water-less).

**Crystal Highway**  Any stretch of poorly-surfaced main road encrusted with sparkling shards of shattered windscreen.

**Culture Vulture**  Carrion-crow companion of the **Arty Farty**. Performer or audient of the lute, viol or racket; *a capella* aficionado; puppet and mime admirer; exhibitionist; provider of a warm hand on your opening.

**Curlypet**  A namby-pamby child: a dated schoolyard taunt. From the name of a proprietary product warranted to produce Fauntleroid curls in the locks of the drabbest suburban babe.

**Currency Lass**  or *Lad*. An Australian-born youngster. Those born at Home were *Sterling*.

**Cut-Lunch Commando**  A gung-ho but desk-bound soldier. Or a member of the Army Reserve. Also: *Weekend Warrior.*

# D

**Dad 'n' Dave**   A comic farming father and son, from the writings of 'Steele Rudd' (Arthur Hoey Davis, 1868–1935). Some of the characters from *On Our Selection* and other collections were used in a long-running radio comedy and a couple of early movies, as well as generations of back-blocks simpleton jokes:

*Dave:* Cripes, Dad, them telephone blokes is silly coots.
*Dad:* Why's that, Dave?
*Dave:* One of 'em just rung up to say it's a long distance from Sydney!

**I.P. Daley**   Author of the schoolyard classic *The Yellow River.*

**Danish Blue**   An unflattering nickname for the Sydney Opera House, designed by Danish architect Joern Utzon. Also called *the Nuns' Scrum.*

**Daphne**   An **Ocker's Sheila**.

**Darling Shower**   Dust storm. Also: *Bedourie Shower; Wilcannia Shower;* a joke extant in most dry and droughty places.

**Dash-hound**   Dachshund, built under licence in Australia. A dog not noted for its dash. Cf. *Rockwheeler; Germ Sheb*—which are also Teutonic *marques.*

**Dead Marine**   An empty beer bottle, casualty of a party or other assault on sobriety.

**The Deep North**   Queensland; for its alleged resemblances, in climate and racial attitudes, to

America's Deep South. **Bananabenders** don't seem to give a **XXXX** about this kind of calumny.

**The Demon Bowler**  Australian Test Cricketer Frederick Robert Spofforth (1853–1926). A terror at detecting the weaknesses of batsmen, the Demon's run-up and delivery of the ball were described as 'a blending of beauty and menace'.

**Diamantina Cocktail**  Isolated but thirsty inhabitants of the Outback, or of the derelict's side of the economic pale, were noted for their concoction of alcoholic drinks from available materials. This says much for the famous Australian talent for invention, and explains the many drink-related deaths of our past. A Diamantina Cocktail consists of a pint of condensed milk, a pint of Bundaberg Rum and a well-beaten emu egg. (The Diamantina River is in outback Queensland.) A *Domain Cocktail* consists of methylated spirits, ginger beer and a dash of boot polish, to taste. (The Domain is a central Sydney park, dormitory for the destitute.)

**Dicky Knee**  An interjecting, insolent schoolboy glimpsed from time to time on the television comedy and variety show 'Hey Hey It's Saturday!'. John Blackman supplies his voice.

**The Digger's Bible**  *Smith's Weekly*, founded in 1919 by Claude MacKay, Clyde Packer and Sir James Joynton Smith. Hailed as 'Truth in trousers!', *Smith's* was a passionate advocate of all things Australian, and the Australian Returned Serviceman (the 'digger') in particular. It was internationally recognised for its comic art. The more sophisticated times following World War Two saw the demise of the tub-thumping paper (d.1950).

**Dinkus**  A word invented in the 1920s by a staff artist of **the Bushman's Bible**, to describe 'spot' drawings, decorative 'flowers', rules, arabesques, vignettes and other typographical 'dividers', like **oooOOOooo**.

**Dinnyhayser**  A **king hit**. From the nineteenth century boxer, Dinny Hayes.

**Dirty Dora**  *Cyperus difformis*, a native sedge which infests the rice crops of Riverina farmers.

**Dismal Guernsey**  A Strine phrase that describes what happened on 14 February 1966: Australia abandoned pounds, shillings and pence (and with them, the duodecimal arithmetic inflicted on schoolchildren for decades) and adopted dollars and cents. This also meant the end of the *trey,* **zac, bob,** *deener* and *quid*. The new notes and coins, with their elegant designs, have attracted no nicknames, though there was a suggestion that the (now withdrawn) 2¢ coin, which had Lillibet Windsor on one face and a frill-necked lizard on the obverse, be called a *twin-lizzie*.

**Dog's Disease**  Influenza.

**The Doll**  Ray Lawler's celebrated play *The Summer of the Seventeenth Doll* (1955), one of the works which wrenched Australian theatre away from the dreary drawing room of British West End tradition and hurled it into a harrowing and thoroughly Australian back yard. Perennially produced by amateur and professional companies alike.

**Dollar Bill**   The one-dollar banknote vanished from the tills and pockets of Australia after 1984, when an aluminium-bronze coin was introduced in its stead. In 1988 the two-dollar bill was also superseded by a coin. The bronze 1¢ and 2¢ coins were withdrawn from circulation from October 1992. In that year the controversial five-dollar note was circulated. It was not only made of plastic, which gave it the look and feel of 'play money', but, despite the republican rumblings of an increasing number of Australians, bore the portrait of Her Majesty, Queen Elizabeth of Great Britain (and at the time, Australia), replacing folk heroine Caroline Chisolm. There was a short-lived campaign mooted to deface the notes and force their withdrawal. **Granny Herald** printed a letter inviting those who objected to the new notes to send them to a given address... See also **Dismal Guernsey**.

**Dolly's Wax**   The point of repleteness, when dining. Dolls once had a body of cloth and a head of wax, so that, figuratively, to be *full up to dolly's wax* is to have stuffed oneself with food up to neck-level. *Up to pussy's bow* is an equivalent and possibly self-explanatory expression.

**The Don**   Famous cricketer, epochal batsman, Sir Donald Bradman (b.1908).

**Don Two**  A would-be ladies' man. Not up to being Don Juan.

**Dorothy Dix**  A set-up question from a backbencher which allows a minister to make a political speech in reply. Dorothy Dix was an American agony columnist, who was rumoured to provide her own 'readers' letters'.

**Drongo**  A person lacking both gorm and feck. Possibly from the 1920s horse of the same name, which never won a race. Also: *Dicrurus bracteatus*, a passerine bird of the coast and tropics; a multipartnered bush dance.

**Drop Bear**  Fabulous inhabitant of the Austral boskage, reputed to drop from the trees upon after-dark pedestrians and hug them to death. A tale invented in WWII to frighten American servicemen camped in the north Queensland rainforest.

**The Drover's Dog**  Canine exemplar of doggedness. A faithful follower, through every variety of vicissitude, who is rewarded with kicks and curses. A phrase used to describe W.E. 'Bill' Hayden, long-serving Labor politician, when he was replaced as leader by R.J.L. 'Bob' Hawke, just before the party won the 1983 national election.

**The Drover's Wife**  Unnamed, for she is Everywoman. Every woman who lived a hard, uncomplaining life with courage and humour, and who remains unknown, but not, perhaps, unsung. From Henry Lawson's celebrated short story of the same name (1892).

**The Drum**  Inside information.

**Duckback Soup**  Scalding-hot soup. If incautiously sipped, it makes you duck back.

**Dud**  No good. A failure; a malfunctioning item.

**Duds**  Trousers.

**Dunrutin**  A famous retirement village.

# E

**Earwig**  An eavesdropper, esp. a child listening to adults' gossip.

**Dame Edna Everage**  A suburban monster, a colossus of *kitsch* and poetess of the numblingly mundane. 'Housewife Superstar' Dame Edna Everage is a creation of the incalculable Barry Humphries.

Dame Edna Everage

**Eggshell Blonde**  A bald Australian.

**Egon Toast**  Author of *Cookery Made Simple*.

**Emma Chissit**  In 1964 British author Monica Dickens was autographing copies of her latest book, in Sydney. A lady thrust a copy under Miss Dickens' nose, and said 'Emma Chissit'. Miss Dickens smiled graciously, and inscribed it *To Emma Chissit*. The customer, looking both annoyed and puzzled, said 'No! Emma *Chissit!*' Miss Dickens, not a Strine speaker, had to have it explained to her that the lady was merely asking the book's price.

**Emoh Ruo**  A popular name for an Australian residence, like **Iona**, *Weona, Meumpi, Kia-Ora* or *Dunromin*. The fashion is somewhat *passé*, save amongst the *arrivistes*.

**Emu Parade**  A campers' clean-up exercise, where everyone walks about stooping to pick up litter, like a feeding emu.

**Ern Malley**  A non-existent Australian poet, figuring in a literary hoax. In 1943 two enemies of Modernism fabricated the works of 'Ern Malley' by writing alternate lines of gibberish, and fooled the editor of the literary journal *Angry Penguins* into printing the material and applauding their 'author'. However, Malley was no McGonigal, and 'The myth is sometimes greater than the creator', said the editor, Max Harris. Sydney Nolan painted Ern's portrait; there are several stanzas of Malley's 'work' and a letter from his 'sister' Ethel, in the *Dictionary of Australian*

*Quotations*; but only one of the hoaxers (James MacAuley) gets a **guernsey** therein.

**Erstwhile**  The erstwhile meaning of 'erstwhile' was 'former; no longer; past'. Judging by its current usage in One Nation, it now means vaunted, courageous, intrepid, versatile, or some such, as used in the phrases *Our erstwhile Club President* or *Your erstwhile newsletter editor.* This is not so much a shift in meaning as a crashing, clutchless change.

**The Ettamogah Pub**  This cartoon creation by Ken Maynard features in his strip *Ned and His Neddy.* The improbable building, tiny and ramshackle, overflows with **Jacky Howe**'d patrons and attracts such oddities as galahs in hobnailed boots and trucks on its roof-ridge. A replica has been built at the real Ettamogah, just north of Albury in southwest New South Wales.

**Ex-Pat**  An Australian, often a practitioner of the Arts, who, in the absence of any encouragement or prospects in his native land, has sought and secured success abroad, thereby incurring the undying contempt of his stop-at-home coevals. See **Tall Poppies**.

# F

**Faceless Men**  The policymakers of the A.L.P., unelected by the community, and by implication, unrepresentative of its opinion and a threat to its well-being. A 1963 taunt attributed to **Ming**.

**Fairy Clap**  Gentle applause, produced by tapping two fingers upon the opposite palm, or with the thumbnails.

**Farn-arkeling**  A vigorous, popular, well-paying and non-existent sport, invented by the punishing John Clark (a.k.a. **Fred Dagg**). His barking, sententious commentaries and absurd interviews satirised sports-obsessed Australia, its egomaniac athletes and its journalist priesthood.

**Fat Cat**  Overpaid and underworked public service mandarin. Also: a mute television puppet moggy.

**Federation Home**  In the rhetoric of real-estate, this refers to a brick-veneer project box with some nailed-on gingerbread, 'leadlights' (coloured panes of glass), microscopic bedrooms and a garage door punched into its façade like a black eye.

**The Ferret**  Nickname of the *Nation Review*, a vigorous and on the whole successful satirical newspaper, published 1972–79, thence as a monthly until 1981. Cartoonist Michael Leunig says that he was once trying to draw a lean and snouty dog when the editor looked over his shoulder and cried, 'That's us! Lean and

Fat Cat

nosy—like a ferret!' and bore off the figure, to become the paper's logo and alter ego.

**Fibergayd**   The emergency service which extinguishes burning buildings. See also **Ambleeance**.

**The Fish**   A commuter train, carrying passengers to Sydney daily from the Blue Mountains, about an hour west of the city. They travel home on **the Chips**.

**Five Finger Discount**   Obtaining goods at the cheapest possible price, i.e. by shoplifting.

**Flake**   Succulent Austral fish, never displayed on the fishmonger's marble. In truth, a battered hunk of shark.

**Flash Fan**   Men *point Percy at the porcelain*; women *flash Fan at the pan*.

**Foo**   The familiar graffito, peering over a brick wall with his long nose. *Foo was here*, runs the caption beneath it. The Australian cousin of the British *Chad*.

**Fred Dagg**   New Zealander John Clarke wrote and performed the satirical monologues of this radio raspberry-blower who delivered short, slangy, rapid-fire, excoriating 'reports' on subjects like advertising, real-estate agents, public servants and Australian politics. Dagg was shorn from the ABC for being 'too political'.

**Foofer Valve**   Device protecting the Australian worker, industrial and domestic, from over-exertion. *'Slow down, son, or I'll bust a foofer valve!'* gasps the grafter, dropping his end of the load and subsiding onto something for a lengthy, panting sit. Also: *Foo-foo valve*.

**The Fremantle Doctor**   A cool refreshing wind, arriving at the end of a hot day, along the coast of Western Australia. The Doctor has practices in Albany and Esperance as well. Cf. **Southerly Buster**.

**Frog Hollow**   The local Lovers' Lane, so-called from the quantity of *frogs* (*French letters* = condoms) to be found there.

**Furphy**   A rumour. John Furphy, brother of Joseph ('Tom Collins') was the manufacturer of a horsedrawn tanker (a *furphy*), which travelled about army camps, its attendant dispensing water and gossip.

**The FX**   The unofficial designation of the first model of the native Holden motor car (correctly, the model 48–215), built at Fishermen's Bend in 1948. General Motors-Holden began the two-letter designation of each model with its *next* car, the FJ, continuing with the FE, FC, FB, EK and so on... Motoring enthusiasts named the first model the FX, in order to refer to it conveniently. These two-letter invocations are part of the arcana of the Australian Male, and any bloke who cannot describe the difference between, say, the EH and EJ model Holden sedans is suspected of being a *poofter*, or worse, a *Pom*.

# G

**Garbo**  Refuse operative. With the advent of machinery-mustered muck (see **Otto**), the football-jerseyed, jog-trotting, bin-bashing, sandshoe'd garbo is a stranger to our streets.

**George**  The Crown; the Government, the bearer of ultimate responsibility; as in the expressions *Let George do it! Let George Pay for it!* (WWII slang, referring to King George VI.)

**The Ghan**  A famous train, which has carried goods and passengers from Port Pirie (S.A.) to Oodnadatta and Alice Springs, in Central Australia, for decades. Named after the Afghan camel drivers who once traversed these lonely parts.

**Ginger Meggs**  A nickname for any red-headed Australian Male. From the comic strip character created by Jim Bancks in 1921.

**Glads**  The flower of the gladiolus, used by Edna Everage as a symbol of Australian philistine suburbinanity.

**Gloria Soame**  The Australian Dream: a house the neighbours envy you for. (Strine.)

**Goanna**  *Varanus varius*, a large lizard of the monitor variety. The word 'goanna' looks Aboriginal but is merely a corruption of the Spanish 'iguana', which the goanna isn't. The Koori word is *perenti*. There is an abundance of misnomers amongst the names of Australian wildlife, which had European names attached to them, just as many towns were named longingly after utterly dissimilar places at

Home. Thus, our *possum* isn't a possum, the *emu* is misnamed from a Portugese word for *ostrich*, the *koala* is not a bear, and the harmless *tarantula* resembles its feared European relative only in having eight legs.

**The Goanna**   A powerful businessman with underworld connections, allegedly the media baron popularly known as 'Australia's Richest Man'. No proof was ever produced to substantiate the allegations, apart from the gentleman's physiognomy, which suggests that the whole affair may have been simply a manifestation of the **Tall Poppy** Syndrome.

**God's Waiting Room**   Surfer's Paradise, Queensland; from the number of retired Australians who have chosen to live there, perhaps due to its much-advertised absence of death-duties.

**Godzone**   God's own country: **A Strayer**.

**Captain Goodvibes**   A gravel-voiced, abundantly aggressive cartoon character, appearing in the surfing magazine *Tracks*, who also shared the airwaves with disc-jockeys Alan McGirvan and Mack Cocker, during the early days of ABC Radio's first all-rock, youth station, 2JJ, circa 1975. A comic strip creation of Tony Edwards, who was also the Captain's on-air incarnation.

**Gozinter**   Schoolteacher; from the arithmetic rule *two gozinter 6 three times*.

**Gozunder**   Chamber-pot, which *gozunder* the bed. More common when most Australian

The Great White Shark

homes were unsewered, to save one a long, cold trip to an outdoor **thunderbox**.

**Granny Herald**  The broadsheet *Sydney Morning Herald* (est. 1831) personified. A prim, bonneted beldame, conservative, but not without a sense of humour, or a sharp eye for nonsense.

**Granny Smith**  A variety of apple, green, crisp and acid, best used for cooking and preserving. First cultivated by Mrs Maria Ann ('Granny') Smith at Eastwood, NSW, in 1860.

**The Great Australian Novel**  The as-yet unwritten blockbusting, world-shaking definitive, all-revealing, summing-up, exposé, kiss-and-tell, panoramic-in-time-and-space work which will nail Australia's literary colours firmly to the mast and its author to a gidgee-wood crucifix.

**Great White Shark**  Blonde, dangerously-good golfer Greg Norman.

**Greenbottle**  Insurgent schoolboy from the 1950's radio comedy series 'Yes What', played by Jack Gardiner. The program was actually made in the 1930s, but repeated—even to this day—around the nation.

**Groperland**  See **Westralia**.

**Grouse**  Not the game bird. An imprimatur of approval:

*Waiter:* How did you enjoy the mud-crab, sir?
*Dad:* Extra grouse. But cripes, the crust was baked a bit 'ard.
(Ancient Dad 'n Dave jape.)

**Grunt**  Footsoldier; front-line trooper, (Services/police force slang). One treated as a faceless, expendable, unambitious ranker.

**G.S.T.**  *Goods and Services Tax*, similar to the Brits' *Value Added Tax*, proposed by Dr John 'I'll Resign If It's Not Adopted' Hewson, Leader of the Opposition, during the 1993 Federal election. The Government won, against all psephological prophecy, Australians apparently being even more afraid of Dr John and his G.S.T. than once they were cowed by **Ming's Yellow Peril** and **Red Menace**.

**Gubba**  A patronising term for a white man. (Koori.)

**Guernsey**  *To get a guernsey* is literally to be given a football jumper, and thereby, a place on the team. The expression metaphorically means 'to succeed'. From the Channel Isle garment of the same name. Also: *Jersey*.

**Gundy**  *No good to Gundy:* an unacceptable circumstance. But who was Gundy? Or does it refer to the town eighty kilometres south of **Nundle**? Or an Aboriginal shelter?

# H

**Hanrahan**   A perennial pessimist; from the comic backblocks poem by 'John O'Brien' (P.J. Hartigan):

*And so around the chorus ran*
*'It's keeping dry, no doubt,'*
*'We'll all be rooned,' said Hanrahan,*
*'Before the year is out.'*

**Happy Jack**   *Pomatostomus temporalis*, the Grey-crowned Babbler.

**Harry's Café de Wheels**   It was never a café, and being a caravan on blocks, it has no working wheels, but this all-nite pie-stall has fed hungry sailors and celebrating Sydneysiders for decades. It has been moved from its pozzie near the Garden Island Naval Dockyard, but isn't far away.

**A Hatful of Arseholes**   Perhaps in the morgue of a teaching hospital such a collection might be found. Otherwise, it exists merely as a pungent simile for the ill-favoured.

**Henley-On-Todd Regatta**   A **Clayton's** regatta, held in Alice Springs in Central Australia. The Todd River is notoriously dry, and the contestants use home-made boats with no bottoms, simply running along the sandy bed of the river carrying their craft.

**Herb**   To travel rapidly, usually in a motorcar. Also: to dispose of violently, as in *'Pwharrr...herb it out the window, it's gone off.'*

**Herby**   Not the Disney Beetle, but nonetheless

55

a motoring adjective to describe a powerful car and/or its engine.

**Hessian Bag**   An ill-favoured mercenary? Not at all: a sack made of jute and or sisal. A.k.a. a *sugar bag*, and very handy for carrying home chooks from the markets.

**Hill's Hoist**   The skeletal carousel of our back yards. Rotary, pyramidal wash-line, invented in 1946 by Lance Hill, and now a suburban icon.

**Hughie**   The munificent Deity, granter of much-needed rain. The grateful farmer turns his wet face skywards, and roars *'Send 'er down, Hughie!'* (from L. Iuppiter Pluvius?)

**Hugo De Buggery**   Fabled proprietor of pubs, restaurants, cafés and other places of refreshment whose true title is uncertain.

**Hungry Mile**   Sussex Street, Sydney. The name was bestowed during the Depression, a time when, as photographs prove, thousands of men wearing hats congregated to look up gauntly at cameras.

# I

**Incentivation**   A 1987 coinage of the Liberal Party; a word to describe the tonic they would fain prescribe for a flagging Western (i.e. our) economy. A hybridisation of *incentive* and *motivation*, it did not get a **guernsey** in our dictionaries.

**Inspector of Schools**   This grey-suited Inquisitor has vanished from classrooms, and the 'sudden death' method of assessment for promotion has given place to 'promotion by merit'. The hopeful teacher no longer has his spirit crushed by some brusque, Departmental hatchet-man. Instead, he faces a panel, which politely crushes his spirit by promoting a brisk woman with shoulder pads.

**Iona**   The name given to many an Australian home where the mortgage has been paid off. See also **Emoh Ruo.**

# J

**Jack**  *Jack of* = fed up with. *Jack up* = to become uncooperative.

**Jack the Painter**  The very cheapest tea leaves, which were reputed to make a brew so potent it stained enamel pans and tinted innards.

**Jacky**  *Sitting up like Jacky* is placing oneself in a prominent and usually undeserved position, with both dignity and impudence. Also: a patronising term for an Aborigine.

**Jacky Howe**  A sleeveless shirt, worn by shearers, truck drivers, labourers, radical Feminists, and others who wish to keep the arms free and the torso cool. Named for the 'gun' who first 'built' it (as they say in the rag trade).

**Jacky Winter**  *Microeca leucophaea*, a well-known garden bird.

**Jake**  Satisfactory. All right, okay. Used in the mysterious, bisexual expression *She's jake.*

**Jerry**  Night crockery. (From *jereboam*?)

**Jerry Built**  Shoddily constructed; or hastily built for temporary use. (From *jury-rig*?)

**Jerry Can**  Oblong, ribbed metal petrol container with moulded handle, robust and wieldy. Copied from German Army, WWII. (*Jerry* = German soldier.)

**Jessie**  An individual with more hide than Jessie is exceptionally thick-skinned, i.e.

bumptious. Jessie was a Taronga Zoo Park elephant, obit. 1939.

**Jimmy Britt**  To defecate. (Rhyming slang.) From the name of a boxing champion. Cf. *Johnny Bliss* = piss.

**Jimmy Woodser**  An alcoholic drink, consumed in isolation.

**Jindyworobacks**  In the late 1930s, a literary movement, founded by writer Rex Ingamells (d.1955), which attempted to 'free Australian art from whatever alien influences trammel it'. Detractors called the 'Jindies' *bushbashing* and *eucalyptusy.*

**Joe Blake**  Any *Ophidian.* (Rhyming slang.)

**Joe Bloggs**  The man in the street. See **Joe Blow**.

**Joe Blow**  The Common Man; the man in the street; usually serving as a hapless or apathetic example. See **Joe Bloggs**.

**Joe Factory**  The average male T.V. audient, as personified by the advertising-driven commercial television industry. The lowest common denominator of the population, whose tastes are assiduously measured and pandered to. The acid-test applied to all scripts coming before a television satrap is *'What's this going to mean to Joe Factory?'* The female of the species is Mrs Mordialloc (from the Melbourne suburb of the same name).

**Joe the Gadget Man**  A popular television personality of the Fifties and Sixties, who demonstrated intriguing, amusing,

Joey

'revolutionary', and sometimes downright absurd household appliances and kitchenware, whilst speaking at top speed in Cockey street-stall patter. Real name: Joe Sandow.

**Joey**   The young of the kangaroo, and by extension, any junior or nobody. Stockmen's camps often had a young boy as their 'wood and water joey'.

**John Dory**   *Zeus australis*, a succulent deep-bodied fish with a minatory countenance. Also: an evil piscine character in the Australian children's classic *Snugglepot and Cuddlepie* (1940) by May Gibbs.

**John Thomas**   See **The Wife's Best Friend.**

**Johnny Cake**   Small wheat-flour cake, made on the coals of a campfire.

# K

**Kangaroo**  Folklore has it that the word *kangaroo*, to describe the well-known macropod, is unknown in any Aboriginal dialect. The story goes that Joseph Banks, on first seeing a boomer bound by, asked incredulously of the nearest native, 'What the devil is that?' The native allegedly replied 'Kangaroo?', meaning *'What did you say?'*, and the word passed, by way of the wealthy young FRS's notebook into the English language. Banks became a cape, a strait, a tree and some Sydney suburbs. Of the puzzled Koori, there is no record but his puzzlement.

**Kangaroo Court**  An impromptu tribunal conducted by one's peers, usually with the intent of finding one guilty. Curiously, not a phrase much used in Australia, where the practice is a national pastime. See **Tall Poppies**.

**Kangaroo Feathers**  Nonsense; impossible.

**Kaniva**  A town in western Victoria, from whence greedy and importunate children are said to hail:

'Kaniva paggeda chips, Mum?'
'Kaniva canna Coke?'
'Kaniva paira in-line skates. . .?'
'Kaniva minute's peace?'

**Kelly**  An axe: *to swing Kelly* = to chop wood.

**Kerr's Cur**  The former Prime Minister, Mr E.G. (Gough) Whitlam used this epithet to describe the leader of the Opposition, Mr Malcolm Fraser, on 11 November 1975, when the **Whitlam Garment** was dismissed from office by the Governor General, Sir John Kerr—a Whitlam appointee. Fraser was invited by Kerr to form a caretaker government, and easily won the general election which quickly followed.

**Kickabucketalong**   Another onomatopoeic, mythical, backblocks purlieu.

**King Hit**   A single, tremendous, fight-finishing punch.

**Kirribilli Curse**   *Parietaria judaica*, a.k.a. Pellitory. A noxious weed whose pollen causes asthma, rhinitis and conjunctivitis, and which is becoming widespread on Sydney's North Shore.

**I.P. Knightly**   Author of the playground paperback *The Rusty Bedsprings.*

**Kylie Mole**   Raucous, bubblegum-twining, semi-literate adolescent, a comic creation of Melbourne comedian Mary-Anne Fahey. Kylie's breathless, gabbled monologues, in an excruciating playground patois, were a feature of Channel Seven's 'Comedy Company' during the late 1980s.

# L

**Lady Blamey** An improvised beer glass, made by cracking the top off a bottle with a red-hot wire. The wife of the famous general told the boys how to do it, and became an eponym.

**Lamington** There are several explanations for the name of this fête and fundraising favourite: that Lord Lamington's cook once dressed up some stale sponge cake with chocolate icing and coconut; that it resembles a similar edible from Leamington Spa; that it's 'laminated', or made in layers. Choose one to taste.

**Larry** A person of exemplary cheerfulness. To be *happy as Larry* is to be heedless and joyful.

**Larry Dooley** Retribution, physical or verbal. (From the boxer Larry Foley, circa 1870?)

**Lasseter's Reef** In 1897 Lewis Bell ('Possum') Lasseter claimed to have found a rich reef of gold, somewhere in the Petermann Range, in Central Australia, and in 1930 convinced an expedition to return with him to rediscover it. It was never located, and Lasseter himself left the party and died in the desert. The reef was probably a myth, but Lasseter was real and colourful enough for author Ion Idriess to extract the best-selling *Lasseter's Last Ride* from.

**Laura Norder** In 1968 when Vietnam war protesters lay down in front of his car, NSW Liberal Premier Robert Askin ordered his driver to 'run over the bastards'. This remark typified his leadership style, and not long after, this graffito appeared in Woolloomooloo: *Bob Askin loves Laura Norder.*

**Left Right Out**   Favoured position for woosie schoolboy rugby players, like the author.

**Leg Opener**   A bottle of wine, which a certain kind of Australian male believes to be a female aphrodisiac.

**Sir Les Patterson**   A gross, beverage-and-banquet-stained braggart, retained by the Commonwealth as a plenipotentiary; a satirico-comic creation of the astonishing Barry Humphries. A horrifying portrayal of far too many Australian politicians, and plenipotentiaries.

**Libby**   Leotarded helpmeet to **Norm**; Libby is fitter, busier and happier than her hulking hubby. A Good Example.

**Lily on the Dustbin**   A woman overdressed for the occasion; a misfit; a wallflower, or *shag on a rock.*

**The Little Boy from Manly**   In the hey-days of **the Bushman's Bible**, the lofty 'Hop' (Livingstone Hopkins) was the king of cartoonists, and he personified a young and growing Australia as a small boy, in a peaked and tasselled cap, often beset by threats like **the Yellow Peril**.

**The Little Digger**   Prime Minister W.M. Hughes (1864–1952), diminutive and pugnacious promoter of Australia and all things Australian; especially devoted to the

Sir Les Patterson

interests of the Australian Serviceman. A Welshman, Hughes was somewhat ill-favoured, having little hair, narrow eyes, prominent teeth, outstanding ears and a huge nose. Whilst viewing a newly painted portrait of Hughes, a friend commented 'It does you justice, Billy.' 'It's not justice I want,' retorted Hughes, 'It's mercy!'

**Little Johnny**   The average child, when used as an example: *What are you going to tell Little Johnny when he asks about AIDS?*

**Little Tin God**   A self-important person, dressed in a little brief authority.

**Logie**   Like Hollywood's Oscar, a statuette awarded by the Australian television industry to itself to recognise its own excellence. A name invented by television personality Graham ('Gra-Gra'; 'The King') Kennedy in 1958; from John Logie Baird, one of the pioneers of television technology.

**LOMBARD**   **L**ots **O**f **M**oney, **B**ut **A** **R**eal **D**ickhead.

**Long Paddock**   The grass at the roadside, available to every impoverished grazier.

# M

**The Man from Ironbark**  A credulous hayseed; a dupe. From the poem by A.B. 'Banjo' Paterson, which describes the visit to town for a shave and a haircut by a back-blocks innocent, who is fooled into believing that his throat has been cut:

*'Murder, bloody murder!'*
*cried the man From Ironbark.*

**The Man outside Hoyt's**  A source of rumours. From a time when cinema houses were embassies of culture and their doormen had an ambassadorial gravity, and a uniform to shame Hermann Göering.

**Mary Pickford**  A very brief wash, 'in three acts' (head, crotch, feet). (Sheilaspeak.)

**Mateship**  The mysterious Australian male manifesto of solidarity. Is it the doctrine of Mateship which cases one man to address another as 'mate', just before he punches his lights out?

**Matilda**  A swagman's roll of blankets, containing his chattels. 'Waltzing Matilda' was the itinerant's sardonic description of his endless, lonely tramping around the countryside in search of work or food. Also a short-lived but promising satirical magazine, published 1985–86, which died of a dearth of advertising and a fusillade of writs.

**Mavis Bramston**  'The Mavis Bramston Show' (1964–68) was a milestone in Australian television comedy and satire. But, save for a few seconds during the opening titles, Mavis Bramston never appeared in the program at all. Toothy, picture-hatted Mavis was personated by Maggie Dence.

*Sit back, relax, forget your income tax,*
*We'll give you all the pertinent facts,*
*Here's Mavis. . .*

**Meehan**   Unit of government expenditure, as in *We're gunna spend eight meehan dollars in the next twelb munce. . .* See also **A Strayer**.

**The Mex**   State Railways abbreviation for the *Melbourne Express*, a train destined for the allegedly uncivilised parts South of the Border.

**Mexicans**   Inhabitants of the State of Victoria, South of the Border. Once known as *Gumsuckers*.

**Mick**   Any adherent of the Roman Catholic Faith.

**Midnight Spares**   Purveyor of stolen automobile parts.

**Min Min Lights**   Mysterious lights, which evade pursuers in the Diamantina and other areas of outback Australia. Are they artesian gas, static electricity, a farmer with a lantern—or dead men's campfires?

**Ming**   Unit of currency suggested by wags to replace the pound, when **dismal guernsey** was in its planning stages.

**Ming Dynasty**   The reign of Prime Minister Sir Robert Gordon ('I am British to the Boot-heels') Menzies, who once explained to the benighted Australian electorate that the correct pronunciation of his Scottish sir-name is *Mingis*, instantly earning himself a nickname to replace **Pig Iron Bob**.

**Mister Completely**   Author of the schoolboy classic *The Hole In My Bed*.

**Mister Dash-and-Dart**   An impatient, dangerous driver, starring in a road-safety short sponsored by B.P. petrol during the 1960s. We see the family sedan, driven by a prudent paterfamilias, overtaken recklessly by a speeding Mr Dash-and-Dart. Eventually, the family arrives safely at **the Three Sisters**, but Mr Dash-and-Dart turns up much later with a dented mudguard. He examines it with dismay, pantomiming remorse by running a chagrined hand through his hair, now too distraught to elbow aside anyone up at the Lookout. This high moral tone has largely evaporated from gasoline advertising.

**Molly Dooker**   A left-handed boxer.

**Mountain Devil**   A shrub *(Lambertia formosa)* which has seed pods resembling a horny little devil's-head.

**Mulga Bill**   Another archetypal clodhopping innocent, like **the Man from Ironbark**, and used by A.B. ('Banjo') Paterson in his ballad 'Mulga Bill's Bicycle'.

**Mullygrubber**   A ball bowled during a cricket match which rolls along the ground without bouncing, making it difficult to score runs off. Frowned upon by serious cricketers, but not unknown amongst tennis-ball elevens.

# N

**Naomi**  Australian Goddess of Financial Embarrassment. Invoked in such prayers as *Naomi backpay, Naomi sick leave, Naomi holiday loading. Naomi an apology, too.*

**The Never-Never**  The enormous, seemingly endless Australian Outback.

**Nino Culotta**  The pseudonymic Italian immigrant who wrote a very funny book about his experiences as a 'New Australian'. *They're a Weird Mob* was perhaps the first close look Australians had taken at themselves and their values since Federation, at least in a popular literary form. *They're a Weird Mob* sold more than half a million copies for its author manqué, John O'Grady.

**Noahs**  Noah's Ark: shark. (Rhyming slang.)

**Nora Titsoff**  Author of the schoolboy best-seller *The Baby's Revenge.*

**Norm**  Big-bellied couch-potato cartoon character, typifying the overweight, indolent and apathetic Australian of the suburbs. Used in the *Life—Be In It* public health campaign.

**Norman Gunston**  a.k.a. *The Little Aussie Bleeder.* A comic character, portrayed by actor Gary MacDonald (b. 1950), Norman Gunston raised gaucherie to the level of an art form, and Australian television comedy to new heights. His interviews with celebrities were excruciatingly—and slyly—inept, and extraordinarily funny. The character was

created by writer Wendy Skelcher for the
ABC's 'Aunty Jack Show', in 1973.

**Nosmo King**  A legendary detester of tobacco
and cigarettes, who advertises himself
pompously, e.g. *Nosmo King In This Building*.

**Nullarbor Nymph**  A feral naked lady
purportedly sighted near Eucla (S.A.) in 1972.
One of the few women not linked romantically
with Prince Charles.

**Nundle**  The sound of a householder retrieving
an **Otto** from the kerbside. Also: a town in
northeastern New South Wales.

# O

**OAF**   **O**ld **A**delaide **F**amily. See **Silvertail.**

**Ocarina**   An Australian oafess. Else, a musical instrument resembling a fist with holes in the knuckles.

**Ocker**   An Australian oaf.

Ocker

**The Old Bus**   The three-engined Fokker aircraft flown across the Pacific Ocean by Sir Charles Kingsford-Smith and crew in 1928. Officially named the *Southern Cross*, now preserved for the nation at Brisbane Airport.

**On His T is the Best Poll I See**   A supposed rebus, decipherable from the picture on the lid of a tin of Arnott's biscuits, which shows a parrot on a T-shaped perch. An urban myth?

**One-Armed Bandit**   A poker-machine.

**One-Eyed Trouser Snake**   The male organ of generation. And decreasingly, veneration.

**ONO**   Neither the Beatles' nemesis, nor a soap powder. An invocation placed at the bottom of a classified *For Sale* advert, often by people who aren't sure what it stands for, which is *Or Nearest Offer*, meaning 'Let's make a deal', meaning the item is probably rubbish. . .

**Oo Flung Dung**   Reputedly Oriental author of the schoolboy favourite *The Spot On The Wall.*

**oooOOOooo**   A typographical Gregorian chant, or dinkus, found amidst the text of squash club newsletters, Carols By Candlelight song sheets and other documents produced by volunteer typists, to show the end of a page or section. With the advent of desk-top punishing and the rustication of the inky Imperial, the ghostly oooOOOooo is gleaming, flicking and vanishing away.

**Oozlum Bird**   An outback species, adept at 'flying backwards, to keep the dust out of its eyes' (says poet W.T. Goodge).

One-Armed Bandit

**O.P.'s**  Popular brand of cigarette: **O**ther **P**eople's.

**O.S.**  **O**ver**S**eas; any portion of the world which isn't **Oz** or **Godzone**.

**Oscar**  Oscar Ashe: cash. (Rhyming slang.) Oscar Ashe was a much-admired melodramatist early this century.

**Otto**  Large, plastic, wheeled suburban garbage bin, designed to be emptied by machinery alone. Hastening the **garbo's** demise. A.k.a. the 'wheely' bin. See also **Nundle**. (Company brand name.)

**Our 'Arbour**  Port Jackson, 'one of the finest harbours in the world', according to First Fleeters Lieutenant Ralph Clark and Captain Arthur Phillip of the British Navy, who ought to have known something about such things. The pride of Sydney, and the envy of less endowed states, one of whose residents composed this impudent paean:

### The Sydneysider's Prayer

*Our 'Arbour, which art in Sydney*
*Good-oh be thy name*
*Thy bridge be done,*
*If not in '30, then in '31*
*Forgive us our swell-headedness,*
*As we forgive those coots in Melbourne*
*Who trespass against us.*
*Lead us not into taxation,*
*For ours is our 'Arbour,*
*Our Bridge and Our Bradman*
*For ever and ever, Amen.*

**Our Glad**   Much-loved soprano Gladys Moncrieff (d. 1976) star of many musical hits of the Australian stage.

**Owen Gun**   A cheaply-produced and effective sub-machine gun, named for its inventor, Evelyn Ernest Owen (d. 1949). By 1944 a grateful government owed Owen royalties of £11 250, but was coolly demanding £8 750 tax in return. **The Digger's Bible** blazed into action, and the tax bill was shot away to a sensible level.

**Oxford Scholar**   A dollar. (Rhyming slang.)

**Oz**   The Great, if not the Greatest, South Land. Also: a satirical magazine of the Sixties, centre of a censorship *cause célèbre*, and like the *Honi Soit* and *Tharunka* of those days, boot camp for future media brigadiers.

# P

**Mrs Palm and Her Five Daughters**
Comforters of the solitary male.

**Paroo Dog**   A rattle, made of fencing wire and tin-can lids, used to herd sheep. From the Paroo, a river in northwest NSW.

**Paroo Sandwich**   A goanna between two sheets of bark. Or a mixture of beer and wine.

**Parramatta**   Parramatta cloth, a whitish woollen cloth, made by convict women at the 'Female Factory' at Parramatta, in the early nineteenth century. Thousands of yards were exported. Possibly our first secondary industry.

**Pat Malone**   Solitarily. To be *on one's Pat* is to be lonely indeed. (Rhyming slang.)

**Paterson's Curse**   A tall, robust blue-flowered weed *(Echium plantigineum)* introduced, by careless white settlers. Like **cactus**, an enemy of pastoralists. Also known as *Salvation Jane, Mrs Freer Weed*, and sometimes sold by Melbourne flower stalls as *Riverina Bluebell*.

**Pavlova**   Dessert confection of meringue, whipped cream and passionfruit, invented in 1935 by chef Herbert Sachse and named by a hotelier in honour of the Russian ballerina.

**Penny Bunger**   A firework, explosive rather than colourful, about the length and circumference of the middle finger and costing one pre-decimal penny. Along with *double-happys, tom thumbs* and *tuppeny bungers*, this ammunition was once for sale around the time of 'Cracker Night' (Commonwealth Day, May 24), bang at the end of the school holidays. Penny bunger took part in mischievous and mutilating enterprises like bunger fights, bunger guns, letter-box demolition, animal harassment, and other amusements now banned by Those Who Know What's Best For Us.

**1930 Penny**   The Royal Australian Mint issued—in error—less than 2 000 of this pre-decimal coin, making it an instant collector's item. Proof sets are rarer than **rocking horse manure**. Generations of Australians have been certain that down the back of Nanna's monstrous Genoa velvet sofa lurks a one-coin fortune. An uncirculated 1930 penny is currently worth $50 000.

**Percy**   The male organ of degeneration. *To point Percy at the porcelain* = to urinate. Cf. **Flash Fan**.

**Phillip McCaverty**   A mate of **Ben Dover**.

**Pig Iron Bob**   The Right Honourable Robert Gordon Menzies, Prime Minister from 1939–41. In 1938, when he was Attorney-General, he enforced the export of B.H.P. pig-iron to Japan, where some Australians suspected that it was being wrought into warships and weapons. The epithet has been credited to left-wing activists Stan Moran, the Rev. Bill Hobbin, and Gwendoline Croft. Menzies attributed it to 'that bastard Moran'.

**Pitt Street Farmer**   A city-based businessman who invests in rural property, usually as a tax-loss. Also: *Collins Street Cockie; Queen's Street Bushie.*

**P.L.P.** **P**ublic **L**eaning **P**ost. A playground objurgation to an invader of personal space: *Get orf! Whadda ya think I am—a P.L.P.?*

**Poeppel's Peg**  In 1879 the surveyor Augustus Poeppel hammered in a peg at what he had ascertained to be the point where the borders of Queensland, South Australia and the Northern Territory meet. The peg has vanished, and it was in the wrong spot anyway, due to a worn-out surveying chain. There is now a brass boss at 'Poepple Corner', 300 metres less west.

**Pony**  Small beer glass, sometimes considered a 'lady's' measure.

**Post and Rail Tea**  Unstrained tea, including stems as well as leaves, which appears to have panels of timber fence floating on its surface.

**Mrs Potts**  A stone-heavy laundry iron, heated on the stove and lifted off with a detachable wooden handle. Also: a cartoon character created by Stan ('For Gawsake Stop Laughing') Cross, of **the Digger's Bible**.

**Pox Doctor's Clerk**  The male version of the **lily on the dustbin**. To be *dressed up like a pox doctor's clerk* is to be ostentatiously or inconveniently well-dressed. And what was a pox doctor? Perhaps a get-rich-quick quack? The proprietor of an early version of the glitzy, gold-curtained 24-hour medical centre, as pioneered by 'The Barry Manilow of Medicine'?

**The Price of Fish**  *What's that got to do with the price of fish?* means *Stick to the subject under discussion*. When was the price of fish an issue? During the Fifties, sententious radio-journalist Eric Baume forced down the price of potatoes. This, I believe.

**Prickly Moses**  *Acacia farnesiana*, or Prickly Mimosa; a 'wattle'.

**Prince Alberts**  Pieces of cloth wrapped around a swaggie's feet, to serve as socks. In mockery of the poverty of Albert, Prince Consort, before he married Queen Unamused.

**Proddy Dog**  A Protestant. Catholic school-child's taunt.

**The Pub with No Beer**  Subject of a rueful country & western song written by Gordon Parsons and sung by the legendary Slim Dusty. The 'real' *pub with no beer* was probably the Taylor's Arms Hotel, in northern NSW.

**Pure Merino**  A **Silvertail**.

**Purple Horror**  Document duplicated by a Fordigraph or 'spirit' duplicator, feared by generations of teachers for its finger-staining stencil, and its rapidly-fading copies.

# Q

**Quinkins**   Spirit people of the Cape York Peninsula. The *Imjim* are malevolent, fanged-and-clawed child-stealers. The stick-like *Timara* are benign, if mischievous child-protectors.

**Quoll**   Our so-called Native Cat, which isn't a cat, but a carnivorous marsupial *(Dasyurid)*, and which is approaching extinction due to the invasion of its environment by feral animals, such as the cat.

# R

**A.G. Raff**   Once upon a time, in offices and manufactories around Sydney Town, new boys and 'prentice hands were ordered to ring a certain phone number and ask *'May I speak to A.G. Raff, please?'* They would then learn that they had dialled Taronga Zoo Park. An initiation rite—one of the milder ones.

**Rafferty's Rules**   Total disorganisation and ad hockery: another dig at the Irish? Actor Chips Rafferty's real name, incidentally, was John Goffage.

**Ratbag**   An eccentric. Or a rodent-control officer's reticule?

**The Raw Prawn**   Despite the prevalence of *sushi* restaurants, the raw prawn is still not a popular item of the Australian diet. *Don't come the raw prawn* says the Australian, scornfully. Elsewhere in the world, one says *Pull the other one, it's got bells on* or *Do you see any green in my eye?*

**Red Menace**   Also: the *Red Bogey*. The long-term threat posed by Communism to the serene, prosperous and in-every-way-admirable Australian way of life. Conservatives assured the public that the Red Menace would rule if they voted Labor. In 1941 Menzies managed to have the Communist Party outlawed for a period, as a 'security measure'.

**Red Ned**   The very cheapest red wine.

**Red Rattlers**   Sydney's ageing fleet of groaning, lurching, suburban railway cars, in

their original livery of Tuscan Red, now giving
way to the smooth, slanty, silver *Tangaras*.
Painted on the side of the ruddy beasts was
the escutcheon and motto of the New South
Wales Train Department: *Orta Regens Quam
Pura Nites*, which means *Newly risen, how
bright thou shineth*, a puzzling tag for a rake of
notoriously grubby rolling-stock.

**Red Shirt**   A flogging. (Convict slang.)

**The Red Steer**   Or the *Red Mare*. Bushfire.

**Regretter**   An officer employed by government
and private organisations, especially of the
huge and impersonal type, to feel remorse on
behalf of its officials for some act of
institutional ruthlessness. The Regretter is only
active in the passive voice, in such phrases as:
*Any inconvenience caused by this decision is
regretted*. Victims must often wonder: '*Regretted
by whom?*' Now they know.

**Richard Cranium**   An objectionable person,
a.k.a. *Dick Head*.

**Ripper Rita**   A vivacious Cockney lady, who
jauntily promoted margarine in a television ad.
The phrase remains in the language as an
expression of delight or approval, as does *A
byordee! I'll take 'er 'ome!'*, the catch-cry of
another commercial.

**Riverina Rig**   Member for the Riverina,
Minister for Immigration during the **Whitlam
Garment**, Al Grassby advocated a flamboyant
style of dress, no more adopted by Australians
than was **incentivation**.

**Robber's Dog**   Apparently a very ugly canine. *He had a head like a robber's dog* = he was remarkably ill-favoured.

**Rock Spider**   Almost the lowest form of life in the criminal's bestiary: at present, it means *child-molester.* Lowest is the *dog*, or informer.

**Rocking Horse Manure**   Like *hen's teeth*: scarce.

**Roger and Bid**   Observant taxi-passengers will meet Roger and Bid, the Pyramus and Thisbe of the flag-fall fleet. Roger and Bid are two buttons, part of a time-saving taxi-radio message system. If the driver wants a job which has been broadcast, instead of shouting into a microphone whilst battling traffic or retailing an anecdote, he fingers Bid. Bid squeaks a number to the cab-company control room. If that cab wins the job, the controller will say so over the radio. The driver then pokes Roger.

**Rollie**   Hand-made (i.e. rolled) cigarette. Once the mark of the Real Man, who smoked severe blends of tobacco like Champion Ruby and Log Cabin, using Zig Zag papers from a packet with an Arab in a fez printed on its front, and a ruler up its side, perhaps for measuring the collar on a **schooner**, or a freshly caught **flake**. The well-tempered Rollie dangles securely from the bottom lip, even whilst its host administers a **king hit**.

**Rolls Canardly**   A decrepit motor car, which goes well downhill, but can 'ardly make it up the other side.

**Ronald Furminger**   The pseudonym adopted by Great-Train-Robbing Brit Ronald Biggs whilst hiding in Melbourne from the Old Bill (or The Filf).

**Round John Virgin**   A worshipper present at the nativity of Jesus Christ. Though unacknowledged in the Gospels, every Australian child knows about him from the carol 'Silent Night':

*. . . Round John Virgin,*
*Mother and child,*
*Holy Infant so tender and mild. . .*

From lustily singing our national song, the same children are certain that:

*. . . our home is dirt by sea.*

**The Royal We**   Mode of address used by monarchs. Republican opinion insists that the only place for the Royal We is down the *Royal Doulton.*

**Ruth**   Australia's patron saint of regurgitation. She is invoked during the sufferer's travails, when he cries *'Ruth! Ruuuuuuuth!'* One can call upon *Ralph,* as well. See also **Bourke**.

# S

**Sacred Acre**   A lawn or other portion of a school or other institution where only the elect—graduates for example—may tread.

**Sadie**   A Cleaning Lady. From the song by pop singer Johnny (afterwards John) Farnham.

**Sam Orr**   An irascible, irreverent, knockabout food critic, whose misanthropic, scarifying, foul-mouthed, erudite and very funny reviews of up-market restaurants—and working-men's cafés—were a popular feature of the defunct *Nation Review*. A *nom de plume* of journalist Richard Beckett (d. 1987).

**Sandgroper**   A **Westralian**.

**Sandy Blight**   Trachoma. Inflammation of the eyes, with granulations. Also: a back-blocks comic strip character created by Eric Joliffe.

**Sandy Stone**   Archetypal suburban bore, a decent citizen, a creature of cliché, homily and habit, every Baby Boomer's older relative, and a serio-comic creation of genius, by the immeasurable Barry Humphries.

**Sanno Man**   Here's an authentic drop of dunny doggerel, from a card deposited around Yuletide on a **thunderbox** seat:

### *The Tactful Workers*

*'67 It's been a drag, the sewer's still not through,*
*Or else we would not, once again,*
*Be sending this card to you.*
*For 'MANY' of our customers we seldom see*
*As mainly through the darkness this task should be.*

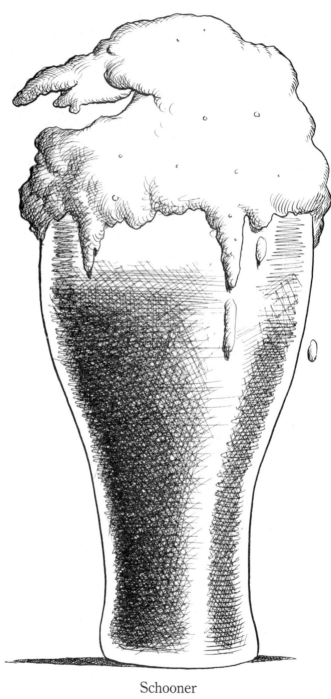

Schooner

*Early—as another dreary day begins,*
*We come to 'LABOUR' with those near full tins,*
*You will find us 'TACTFUL' as we go about our*
*work*
*If behind a closed door a customer should 'LURK'*

*Through the 'WINTER'S' cold and 'SUMMER'S'*
*heat,*
*We still battle through many a long street,*
*Always risking a touch of the 'flu*
*Endeavouring to keep this service up to you.*

*So 'WHEN' the sewer comes in '1974'*
*You may wonder what's become of the men of days*
*of yore*
*And often in the still of night awake in doubt*
*Did you open the B—— gate or are the dogs still*
*out.*
*Now from my 'MATE'—'MYSELF' and all the rest*
*We still 'EXTEND' to you all 'THE BEST'*
*We wish 'YOU' all good cheer*
*Throughout the FESTIVE SEASON and*
*NEW YEAR.*

—Your sanno men

**Schooner**   A **Waler's** large glass of beer.

**Seventeen Door Sedan**   Chariot of the
**sanno man**. It had rows of hatches along its
sides, to accommodate the 'honeypots'.

**The Sex**   State Railways abbrevation for the
*Sydney Express*, considered an apposite
identification for a train heading to the nation's
reputed Sin City.

**Shagger's Back**   Lumbar discomfort, allegedly

from over-achievement at the bedtime game of *Hide the Sausage.*

**Sheila**  Any human female.

**Shit Creek**  Watercourse of misfortune. *Up shit creek in a barbed-wire canoe without a paddle* = in dire straits.

**Show Pony**  Ostentatious dresser, or one who seeks the public eye.

**Shrdlu**  The Australian suburb drawn by cartoonist Emile Mercier. Everyone's Australia, especially not-over-affluent Australia, dirt-tins-in-the-back-alley Australia, tired-housewife Australia, ripped-and-burnt-at-the-dogs Australia. SHRDLU spells out a row of keys on a newspaper linotype machine.

**The Silent Cop**  The British stodgily call it a *traffic dome.* A low bollard, placed at the centre of an intersection, to mark its mid-point and encourage motor cars to make tidy—or at least legal—right-hand turns. With the introduction of the 'diamond turn', the Silent Cop was transferred to scrap-heap duties.

**The Silver Bodgie**  Erstwhile Prime Minister R.J.L. (Bob) Hawke, whose argent hair became increasingly wavy and immaculately coiffed as he climbed the ladder of fame and success.

**Silvertail**  The well-born, well-heeled, well-connected Australian, as described by his ill-bred, ill-used, ill-natured countryman, or *coppertail.*

**Sin City**  Sydney, as once described by the jealous denizens of other states which had nothing to compare with the fabled King's Cross.

**Sixty Miler**   From the late nineteenth century, small ships sailed the sixty sea-miles from Newcastle to Sydney, bringing coal for the city. The export trade is now more important, and natural gas is the favoured fuel. The *Camira*, the last of the Sixty Milers, left Sydney Harbour for Singapore early in 1993.

**Skerrick**   A negligible quantity:

*Shane:* Got any grog left?
*Wayne:* Not a skerrick.
*Shane:* Got any dosh left?
*Wayne:* Not a **brass razoo**.
*Shane:* Bugger it.

**Skippy**   Nickname for white Australians, bestowed by those of 'ethnic' origin. (derog.) From 'Skippy the Bush Kangaroo', the intelligent marsupial star of the eponymous children's television series. Similarly, *Sullivan*, from a long-running TV soap about a thoroughly Ozified family.

**Sleeper Cutter**   A freelance, licensed timber-getter; an expert axeman. The use of the concrete sleeper by state rail authorities, along with pressure from environmentalists, has put his ilk out of work. In 1991 some of Australia's last sleeper cutters were engaged in a struggle with the NSW Government for redundancy compensation.

**Smart Alec**   A person who is offensively knowledgable; or simply offensive; or knowledgable.

**Snake Charmer**  A length of #8 fencing wire, one end twisted into a handle. Used to kill **Joe Blakes** (a protected species) with a smart whipping stroke.

**Snake Gully**  The home of **Dad 'n Dave**. A mythical back-blocks burg.

**Snarler**  **S**ervices **N**o **L**onger **R**equired. Document issued to discharge an undesirable from the Armed Forces.

**Sorry**  The obeisance false. In truth, it means *Up you Jack*. As in: *Look, sorry, but I feel I have to say. . .*

**Southerly Buster**  Refreshing wind, sometimes accompanied by a thunderstorm and rain, blowing over Sydney after a fierce summer day (known as a 'stinker').

**Sparrowfart**  Dawn, or an event occurring adjacent to the crack thereof.

**The Speewah**  Mythical outback station, where there were giants in the earth. There are many tales of *Crooked Mick of the Speewah*, a paragon bumping Paul Bunyon and Baron Munchausen into the Reserve Grade.

**Stewed Roodleums**  A nonsense reply to a nagging child:
'What's for dinner?'
'Stewed roodleums.'
'Err. Yuk.' (Familyspeak.)

**The Sticks**  The backblocks, remote from **the Big Smoke**. Also: *the Ulu, the Boondi, the Booay, Back o'Bourke.*

**Stockman's Dinner**  A smoke and a spit. A *Dingo's Dinner* is *a piss and a look around.*

**A Strayer**  A home girt by sea.

**Strewth**  An Elizabethan oath, meaning *God's Truth*—a commodity in short supply.

**Stubbies**  Shorts (American = *Bermuda shorts*) with an elastic waist and roomy legs. Very popular with active if un-chic men, and those with an expanding waistline.

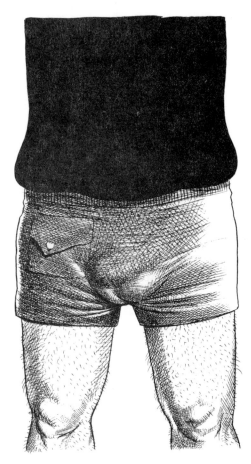

Stubbies

**Stubby**   Squat bottle of lager. Fist-sized; thirst-sized.

**Stubby Holder**   Not, as it seems, a jockstrap. A polystyrene sleeve for a **stubby** which keeps the bottle cold as one stands with the ensemble in one's hand, chatting, at a **barbie**.

**Stu Vac**   Stu's arrival is eagerly awaited by candidates for public examination. Abbreviation for **study vacation**.

**The Sux Family**   Indefatigable dynasty of graffitists. *Wayne Sux, Wanda Sux, Jason Sux, Sheree Sux*, and lately, *Farook Sux* and *Ng Sux* are all well-known bylines in the People's Media: walls, the seats in railway waiting rooms, bus-shelters, and school desk-top publishing.

**Sweet Fanny Adams**   A negligible quantity; a poor outcome. A solecism for *Sweet F. . . All.*

**I.P. Swift**   Author of the schoolboy shortlister *Running Waters.*

**The Sword**   *The Royal Order of the Sword* is awarded to recognise a state of being beyond repair or reclamation.

*Mechanic:* Mate, your motor's had the sword.
*Motorist:* Go to buggery. How much?
*Mechanic:* To the hilt.

**Sydharb**   The amount of water which it is estimated can be held by Sydney Harbour. The capacity of dams is informally measured in Sydharbs.

# T

**Tall Poppy**   Any person who has distinguished themselves in any way. Those eminently successful, and therefore eligible to be summarily cut down to size by an *auto-da-fé* held in the name of our sacred Australian egalitarianism.

**Tantanoola Tiger**   In the wee hours of one 1889 morning, a youth walking home in this South Australian town thought he saw a tiger leap over a fence, with a sheep in its jaws. Police later shot a large wild dog, but stock continued to disappear. A local was later jailed for sheep-stealing.

**Taswegians**   Inhabitants of the state of Tasmania. Phillip Adams has described our island state, which seems to hang from the groin of the mainland, as *the testicle of Australia*. Sir Les Patterson refers to the female pudendum as *the map of Tasmania*. See also **The Apple Isle**.

**Technicolour Yawn**   The act of vomiting.

**Telegraph Pole**   The Overland Telegraph connected Australia to the rest of the world in 1872, but the telegraph as a major form of communication was outdated when the wireless arrived. Nonetheless, those crucifixes of the suburban street, which now carry mostly electricity cables and signs announcing a garage sale, GUESS WHOSE FORTY TODAY JANINE, or the candidature of some municipal rapscallion, are still known as telegraph poles. They take their revenge for this misnomer by suddenly leaping out in front of drunken drivers.

**Theresa Green**  School playground catch, as follows:

*Joy:* Do you know Theresa Green?
*Roy:* No.
*Joy:* Geeze, youse must be dumb if you dunno trees are green!

**The Three Sisters**  Spectacular sandstone outcrop at Katoomba, in the Blue Mountains. Much-photographed tourist spot, and subject of an Aboriginal legend. There are in fact five sisters, though the other two are dwarfs. Cf. *The Twelve Apostles.*

**Throwdown**  Bottle of lager, smaller than a **Stubby**; a measure quickly drained, after which the container is often cast to the ground, unfortunately. *Not* christened by the breweries.

**Thunderbox**  A lavatory, especially the outdoor, sentry-box species. *'Where a man can fart in peace',* as my Uncle John declares. Cf. *Thunderbags* = underpants.

**Tim and Debbie**  Terminally blasé, but totally committed, Tim and Debbie hosted 'Brain Space', an idea-illogically correct segment of the ABCTV comedy program 'Australia, You're Standing In It' (1986). Tim and Debbie nitwittedly opined about matters of vital importance—women, the environment, unemployment, public transport, Christmas—in the morose, world-weary tones and paralytically euphemistic argot of the Alternative Culture.

Written and performed by Steve Blackburn and Mary Keneally.

**The Tintookies**  Puppeteer Peter Scriven created the Tintookies and in 1956 made a highly successful tour with them. *Tintookie* is an Aboriginal word for a kind of pixie, and it applied only to the characters in the first production of the same name. Other popular shows included 'Little Fella Bindi' and 'The Magic Pudding'. Most of the original Tintookie puppets were destroyed by fire in 1969. The others have been stored in tea-chests since 1976, when large-scale marionette productions went out of fashion.

**Tom Bowler**  Large marble; a Schwarzenegger taw. For skite, rather than fight.

**Tom Collins**  A mythical identity, the source of **furphys**. It was the *nom-de-plume* chosen by author Joseph Furphy, (*Such Is Life*, 1903), who did *not* give us the word **furphy**.

**Toolache**  Not a concomitant of **shagger's back** or **brewer's droop**. A rare or perhaps extinct wallaby, *Macropus greyi*.

**Top Enders**  Inhabitants of Australia's newest state, the Northern Territory.

**T'othersider**  Any person living in the Eastern States, on the other side of the Nullarbor Plain. **Sandgroper** slang.

**Touses**  An extremely ragged nether garment. Literally, *trousers* with their *r's* out.

**The Town Bike**  Everyone's had a ride.

**Townie**  The countryman's term for the wily,

sophisticated, but on the whole pitiable, inhabitants of any settlement, from hamlet up to city.

**Cyclone Tracey** *'Santa never made it into Darwin . . .'* goes one lachrymose country & western song commemorating the cyclonic storm which hit the city of Darwin on 25 December 1974, leaving thousands homeless and killing fifty. One of Australia's worst natural disasters. Controversial meteorologist Clement 'Wet' Wragge began giving cyclones female names in 1887, to publicise the work of the Weather Bureau. The practice was ideologically corrected during the term of the **Whitlam Garment**; cyclones are now named after both genders.

**Triantiwontigongelope** An odd creature in a poem for children by C.J. *(The Sentimental Bloke)* Dennis. Incidentally, a *triantelope* is a *tarantula*, which is really a huntsman spider, and a *tryanthewontigong* is a *thingamebob, whatchamacallit* or *hoojah*.

**Tumba-bloody-rumba** The place where, according to some verses of John O'Grady, one shoots *kanga-bloody-roos*. His satirico-comic poem 'Integrated Adjective' laughs at an absurd Australian pro-bloody-pensity for inserting an impre-bloody-cation wherever possible, in the tradition established by C.J. Dennis's *The Austral---aise* and W.T. Goodge's *The Great Australian Adjective!*. (Tumbarumba is a country town in S.E. bloody New South Wales.)

**The Twelve Apostles** A number of monoliths, their feet in the surf, along the coast of southern Victoria. There are in fact only eight Apostles, just as Ninety Mile Beach is only 70 miles long; the only accurate measurement that matters is the click of the tourism turnstile. Also: *a flock of choughs, babblers,* or even *apostle-birds.* Cf. **The Three Sisters**.

**Two-Bob Watch** If you're *as silly as a two-bob watch*, then you're erratic and unreliable. Electronic timepieces are extremely cheap, and fairly reliable, but for the moment cost more than twenty cents.

**Two Pot Screamer** A cheap drunk. A *pot* is yet another name for a beer glass.

**Two-Up School** Floating gambling institution, officially against the law, or at least its letter. Two-up, 'swy', gambling on a brace of tossed pennies, is by tradition tolerated amongst old soldiers by police on 'the one day of the year'—Anzac Day.

# U

**U-Jack Society**   Article of the solemn
Australian **mateship** charter, wherein it is
written, *Up you, Jack: I'm all right.* (From *The
U-Jack Society* by Ian Moffitt, 1972.)

**Uncle Willy**   Silly. (rhyming slang)

**Underground Mutton**   A wry appellation for
a rabbit, an item of diet not unobtainable in
the Australian countryside.

# V

**Victa Mower**   Suburban assassin of
tranquillity, invented by Merv Richardson in
1952, so that his wife could attack the
insurgent paspalum in their back yard. In
cohorts with the whippersnipper, the chain
saw, the trail-bike, the outboard motor and the
jet-ski, it mounts a ferocious, two-stroke assault
upon the declining silence of our suburbs.

**Vinnie's**   The second-hand clothing
'opportunity' shops run by the St Vincent De
Paul Society. Victorians are catered for by 'The
Brotherhood'—the Brotherhood of St Laurence.
(While in Ireland recently, the author saw a
coin-box on a pub counter, which bore the
following entreaty:
*'Mill Hill Missions. Give To God! He Will
Repay! Help St Joseph's Missionary Society works
in Africa, India, Pakistan, Borneo, Phillipines,
Falkland Islands, South America and New
Zealand . . .'*)

# W

**Wait-a-While**  A rainforest climbing palm *(Calamus radicalis)* having many hooks which detail a traveller's clothing, and consequently the traveller.

**Walers**  New South Welshpersons.

**Walter Plinge**  Thespian pseudonym, used in the cast list by an actor wishing to remain anonymous, or when a role is played by a number of actors in the same production.

**Wattle**  Various species of *Acacia*. Limbs from these golden-blossomed trees were used by early settlers to build crude *wattle and daub* huts. A 'wattle' is simply a wand or withy taken from any suitable tree, and woven in combination with daubs of mud to build a wall or fence.

**Wattle Bark**  Every Australian child knows that the correct spelling of this substance is D-O-G.

**The Welcome Stranger**  A huge gold nugget, found on the Victorian goldfields in 1869. It was about the size of a ham-hock, and weighed 2 520 oz. Its finders received £9 500 for their efforts.

**Westie**  Literally, any resident or indigene of the western (less affluent) suburbs of Sydney. Figuratively, a member of the underclass.

**Westralia**  Australia's largest and westest state, called, with minimalist brilliance, Western Australia. Or W.A.

**Wheelbarrow**   Any unknown word, usually when encountered in print. The reader substitutes the word 'wheelbarrow', and continues reading aloud, to keep the flow. Comprehension of text optional. Also: *watermelon word.*

**Whelan the Wrecker**   A famous Sydney demolition firm. A nickname given to a clumsy person.

**Whistleblowers Anonymous**   An organisation started in 1992 by retired public servant (and former Baptist minister) John MacNicol, to expose fraud and corruption in Australia's Public Service.

**White Australia Policy**   Just as Australia has never had a written constitution or bill of rights, so it has never had a published 'White Australia Policy'. Our xenophobia dates back at least to the fear of rivalry from the Chinese who came to dig for gold—the original **Yellow Peril**. The 'letter' of the Immigration Act of 1901 was to exclude political, criminal and social 'undesirables'—those diseased or handicapped, for example—but its 'spirit' was to maintain Australia's Anglo-Saxon homogeneity.

**White City**   Australia's racist penchant hasn't carried it quite so far, yet. White City is a complex of courts in eastern Sydney, headquarters of the New South Wales Lawn Tennis Association.

**White Lady**   Methylated spirits. The tipple of the derelict.

**White Leghorn**   A lady lawn-bowler. From the thick, white stockings which form part of their uniform.

**White Shoe Brigade**   An epithet to describe a group of supporters of populist Queensland premier Joh Bjelke-Petersen, from their used-car-tycoon mentality and dress code: high-candlepower shirt, chunky cufflinks, powder-blue strides, white leather shoes and belt, and pugnacious aftershave. The men were just as gaudy.

**Whitlam Garment**   The reformist administration of the Federal Labor Government, 1972 *(It's Time)* to 1975 *(Shame, Fraser, Shame; Cheats Shouldn't Prosper)*, led by Edward Gough ('Maintain Your Rage') Whitlam. A.k.a. the *Whitlam Camelot Years.*

**Wicked Which of the Rest**   The Wicked Which is ever at the elbow of gabbling One Nationers, waiting for them to saunter into a *which* cause, upon which she casts her colloquy-confounding hex, which they then fumble the rest of the sentence.

**Widgie**   Female **bodgie**. But not Hazel Hawke.

**Widow Tree**   The grey gum *(Eucalyptus punctata)* which has a habit of shedding branches suddenly and killing timber-getters.

**The Wife's Best Friend**   To *shake hands with the wife's best friend* is a male phrase describing masculine micturation.

**Wigwam for a Goose's Bridle**   A nonsense response to a nosey child of the Baby Boomer era.

White Shoe Brigade

*Child:* What's that in your bottom drawer, Mum?
*Mother:* (Flushing) A wigwam for a goose's bridle and go to blazes out of here. (Familyspeak.)

**The Wild Colonial Boy**   The archetypal bushranger: hero to the underdog, untameable foe of authority, victim of society, etcetera. Also: a rather maudlin Australian folksong, supposedly based on the life and exploits of 'Bold' Jack Donahoe, shot dead by police in 1830.

**The Wild White Man**   Escaped convict William Buckley, who was kept alive by Aborigines from 1803 to 1835. He is also a candidate for the origin of the expression *to have Buckley's chance*, but since this Buckley had 32 years' worth of chances, it seems unlikely.

**Willie Jump**   Author of *The Suicide.*

**Willie Wagtail**   *Rhipidura leucophrys*, a restless, chattering flycatcher, familiar to every Australian back yard.

**Willy Willy**   or *Dust Devil.* A micro-cyclone, which seems to meander along collecting debris to fling spitefully at the eyes of bystanders. The Aborigines believed that willy-willys were the spirit of a witch-doctor. They may be right.

**Wilson Supermarts**   A place of employment during the taxable year of 1976/77 of one John James Citizen, of 32 Warrang Crescent, Ashfield. John, a mild-mannered clerk, used to be with H&Q Products Limited, but moved on in '75, probably goaded by wife Mary Jane. They owed a few **bob** to the XYZ Home Finance Company, and she was probably **jack** of dealing with any more firms hiding behind letters of the alphabet.

**Wombat** Any uncouth male, whose relationships with women are those of a burrowing marsupial: he eats roots shoots and leaves. See also **Chaffcutter**.

**Wonk** Contemptuous Aboriginal term for a white man.

**Wooden Spoon** Just as the suburban 21-year-old is awarded a giant wooden key to symbolise adulthood, so a troublemaker or loudmouth is presented with a huge wooden spoon, recognising them as *the World's Biggest Stirrer.*

**Woop Woop** Another mythical back-blocks settlement, a byword for remoteness.

**The Workers' Party** A political party founded by John Singleton and others in the early 70s, with an extreme platform including untrammelled free-enterprise and the abolition of all social welfare. Electorally unsuccessful, it was nonetheless an effective ginger-group. Singleton later said that the Workers' Party became redundant because the major parties adopted his philosophies.

**Wowser** A killjoy; a puritan; not an abstainer merely, but a sour censor of the pleasures of others. A coinage boasted by the muck-raking (and muck-making) proprietor of the *Truth*,

John Norton (1862–1916). Norton was once horse-whipped in Pitt Street by an umbraged politician. This kind of thing doesn't happen to press barons any more.

**J.M. Wright**   The first Bankcard user in Australia, if the 1974 advertising material is to be believed.

# X

**XXXX**  Supposedly the way **Bananabenders** spell the word 'beer'.

# Y

**Yellow Peril**  The Asian Invasion which Australians have dreaded for over a century. The Yellow Peril was to arrive from China, by means of the *Domino Theory*, a scenario that showed how, one by one, South East Asian countries to our north would topple to communism, with Australia as the final—plum—conquest. The Domino Theory apparently did not include Macquarie Island or Antarctica.

**Yowie**  Along with the **Bunyip**, Australia has other monsters, like the *Moha Moha*, and the *Moolooloobah Monster*. The Yowie is a kind of Big Foot, a hairy ape-like man who wanders the **sticks**.

# Z

**Zac**  A sixpence. See **Dismal Guernsey**.

# SELECT BIBLIOGRAPHY

Appleton, Richard (ed.) *The Australian Encyclopedia*, Australian
Geographic, Terrey Hills, NSW, 1988.

Arthur, J.M. & Ramson, W.S. (eds.) *W.H. Downing's Digger
Dialects*, Oxford University Press, in assoc. with The
Australian War Memorial, Melbourne, 1990.

Baker, Sydney J. *The Australian Language*, Sun Books,
Melbourne, 1970.
*The Drum; Australian Character and Slang*, Currawong,
Sydney, 1965.

Beckett, Richard *The Dinkum Aussie Dictionary, by Crooked
Mick of the Speewa*, Child & Henry, Brookvale, NSW, 1986.

Buzo, Alexander *Glancing Blows: Life and Language in
Australia*, Penguin, Ringwood, Vic., 1987.
*The Young Person's Guide to the Theatre (And Almost
Everything Else)*, Penguin, Ringwood, Vic., 1988.

Chisholm, Alec, H. (ed.) *The Australian Encyclopedia*, Grolier,
Sydney, 1963.

Davies, Taffy *Australian Nicknames*, Rigby, Melbourne, 1977.

Delbridge, Arthur, et al (eds.), *The Macquarie Dictionary*, The
Macquarie Library, Sydney, 1981.

Factor, June *Captain Cook Chased a Chook—Children's Folklore
in Australia*, Penguin, Ringwood, Vic., 1988.

Fearn-Wannan, W. *Australian Folklore*, Lansdowne Press,
Melbourne, 1970.

Harris, Max *The Australian Way With Words*, William
Heinemann, Richmond, Vic., 1989.

Hornadge, Bill *The Australian Slanguage; A Look at What We
Say and How We Say It*, Cassell, North Ryde, NSW, 1980.

King, Jonathon *The Other Side of the Coin*, Cassell, Sydney,
1979.

Keesing, Nancy *Lily on the Dustbin* (Shielaspeak; Familyspeak),
Penguin, Ringwood, Vic., 1982.

Lauder, Afferbeck *Fraffly Strine Everything*, Ure Smith,
Sydney, 1969.

Meredith, John *Dinkum Aussie Slang* (Rhyming Slang),
    Kangaroo Press, Sydney, 1991.
Morris, Edward E. *Morris's Dictionary of Australian Words*,
    Viking O'Neil, Ringwood, Vic., 1988.
Murray-Smith, Stephen *The Dictionary of Australian Quotations*,
    Heinemann, Richmond, Vic., 1984.
Turner, I., Factor, J. & Lowenstein, W. *Cinderella Dressed In
    Yella*, Heinemann, Richmond, Vic., 1982.
Weller, Sam *Bastards I Have Met*, Sampal Investments,
    Charters Towers, 1976.
Wilkes, G.A. *Australian Colloquialisms*, Sydney University
    Press, Sydney, 1978.

# FANTASTIC ODDSTRALIANS

## Key

| | | |
|---|---|---|
| 44. Come-By-Chance | 57. Gogo | 70. Gundy |
| 45. The Risk | 58. Pearshape | 71. Nundle |
| 46. Chittering | 59. Punchbowl | 72. Robin Hood |
| 47. Chorkerup | 60. Snug | 73. Smokers Bank |
| 48. Cheepie | 61. Success | 74. Styx |
| 49. Clackline | 62. The Patch | 75. Trundle |
| 50. Darraweit Guim | 63. Walkaway | 76. Useless Loop |
| 51. Goodnight | 64. Winkie | 77. Wards Mistake |
| 52. Humpty Doo | 65. Yea | 78. Whim Creek |
| 53. Indented Head | 66. Amen Corner | 79. Winda Woppa |
| 54. Officer | 67. Jiggalong | 80. Yo Yo Park |
| 55. Nevertire | 68. Dum Dum | 81. Wandering |
| 56. Nildottie | 69. Jinglemoney | |